# Phantom Encounters

MYSTERIES OF THE UNKNOWN

# Phantom Encounters

*By the Editors of Time-Life Books*

TIME-LIFE BOOKS, ALEXANDRIA, VIRGINIA

# CONTENTS

# A Ghost-Ridden Realm

The very word *ghost* conjures up a shadowy, vaporous figure and calls to mind any number of places such a phantom might choose to haunt: graveyards on moonless nights, misty moors, fog-shrouded castles perched high on craggy hills. Such places seem to hold closely guarded secrets of the past and are endowed with an atmosphere of sorrow and foreboding.

To be sure, not all reported phantom encounters occur in such disquieting locations. But tales of ghosts that favor mysterious sites are the most enduring. And just as enthralling as their dramatic habitats are the ways in which the spirits are said to announce their presence. Many people recounting ghostly visits describe a drop in the surrounding temperature just before the ghost appears, or a thickening of the atmosphere—as if, according to one observer, "the room seemed to get very full of people." Others tell of hearing voices or footsteps where no one is present, seeing strange lights, or smelling distinctive odors, such as tobacco.

Photographer Simon Marsden did not experience any of these sensations as a child growing up in two allegedly haunted houses in the English countryside. But he did become fascinated with ghosts. In 1974 he decided to chronicle in pictures some of the thousands of phantoms said to inhabit the British Isles, reputedly the most haunted region in the world. Marsden spent twelve years visiting and photographing almost 1,500 sites. Images from five of the locations, shot with infrared film to evoke an appropriately eerie atmosphere, appear on the following pages.

# The Wraiths of Wilton Castle

Looming above the landscape of southeastern Ireland, only fire-scarred walls remain of once-stately Wilton Castle. Until it was ravaged by flames in the early 1920s, this rambling structure was home to generations of the Alcock family, prominent in the region since the early seventeenth century. If local legends are to be believed, a fair number of ghosts are now harbored within the castle walls.

One story recounts strange lights that are sometimes seen in the remnants of a castle tower where an old woman, a one-time actress, died in a fire. Another tale has it that every year on the anniversary of his death, the shade of Harry Alcock, who died in 1840, is seen driving slowly away from the castle in a ghostly carriage. Crowds once gathered in anticipation of the event, and a local shoemaker claimed to have spoken with the phantom.

The strangest tale, however, is that of neighbor Archibald Jacob, who served as a magistrate and captained a local militia company at the time of the rebellion against Britain in 1798. Jacob flogged and tortured many people in the parish. While returning home from a ball at Wilton Castle one evening in 1836, he was killed by a fall from his horse. For years afterward, his ghost was said to haunt both the scene of his death and the castle. On one occasion, a Catholic priest was summoned to the castle to conduct an exorcism. When he made the sign of the cross, the ghost of Archibald Jacob allegedly appeared in the fireplace, then disappeared in a cloud of smoke.

# Reaching Out from a Watery Grave

Since earliest times, spirits have often been associated with water, whether a rock-fanged coast, a tumultuous river, or an idyllic pool. Some of them are said to be the ghosts of people who have drowned, and these spirits allegedly entice other hapless victims to join them in their watery bowers. In Devon, England, at Lydford Gorge, there exists a dark pool of water fed by a twenty-foot cascade; known as Kitty's Steps, this cataract is said to contain such a seductive spirit.

The story holds that an old woman named Kitty was returning home from market one day many years ago. Rather than follow the main road, Kitty led her horse down a shortcut through a ravine. The narrow pathway took the woman close by the waterfall, where she had played as a child. Recent heavy rain may have made the path slippery, or, as some believe, a spirit may have beckoned to Kitty from the pool. In any event, Kitty never reached home and was presumed drowned. Her horse was found quietly grazing on the riverbank; a red kerchief that she had worn around her head was discovered near the pool. Since then, Kitty's apparition has been reported standing near the waterfall, her kerchiefed head bowed, staring into the water.

In 1968, the pool—or, some say, the water spirit—claimed another victim. A young soldier who was hurrying back to his camp also used the shortcut through the ravine; he was missing for several weeks before his body was found floating on the water's surface below Kitty's Steps.

# The Specter That Stalks Creech Hill

Creech Hill, near Bruton in Somerset, England, was once the site of an ancient Romano-Celtic temple where, in the late eighteenth century, amateur archaeologists uncovered two crossed skeletons, thought to be those of a Norman and a Saxon. Apparently the scene of brutal confrontations long ago, the area is also said to have a long history of hauntings. A number of people traveling at night over the hill or near it have reported the sounds of heavy footsteps and strange laughter, and some have told of seeing a black ghostly shape.

One night, it is said, a farmer returning from a nearby market stumbled upon a figure lying in the road at the foot of Creech Hill. Suddenly the figure rose to a commanding height and let out a bone-chilling shriek. The terrified farmer fled for home, with the dark specter close on his heels. When he burst through his front door and collapsed across the threshold, his stunned wife caught a glimpse of a long black figure bounding away in the direction of Creech Hill, laughing crazily.

In yet another account of the Creech Hill phantom, a man, armed with a lantern and a stout hazel stick, ventured across the hill one night to keep an urgent appointment. Halfway through his journey, he encountered a deadly coldness, and then something tall and black rose up from the ground before him. Startled, the man struck out at the hideous shape, but the stick passed right through it; he tried to flee but found himself rooted to the spot. Peals of maniacal laughter deafened the traveler as he swung wildly at his tormentor again and again. Not until the first light of dawn appeared did the apparition vanish, leaving its victim free to move once more.

# A Phantom with a Deadly Drink

One of the earliest ghosts reported in the British Isles is said to haunt an ancient burial mound at the Manor of Rillaton, located on a moor in Cornwall. The ghost, apparently a Druid priest dressed in a long flowing robe, would approach passersby and mutely offer them a drink of a magic brew.

According to one account, a local nobleman encountered the phantom late one night while riding across the moor after a day of hunting. As he passed the mound, the figure of a frail old man with a vacant stare and pallid complexion walked toward him, clutching a golden cup. Silently he extended the vessel as if to offer a drink. The nobleman hesitated at first, feeling an inexplicable chill envelop him, but he gave in to his thirst and drained the cup.

Or so he thought. When the nobleman lowered the cup, some liquid remained. Again he drank deeply. And again the liquid reappeared. Enraged by what he saw as the mysterious figure's trickery, the nobleman flung the liquid into the stranger's face and dropped the cup at his feet. Still the robed figure remained silent, a strange, sardonic smile crossing his face. At that, the nobleman spurred his horse and rode for home, deeply concerned over what his meeting with the ghostly stranger might portend. A few days later, both the nobleman and his horse were discovered dead at the bottom of a nearby ravine.

Years later, in 1837, when archaeologists began excavating the burial mound at the Manor of Rillaton, they made an intriguing discovery: A skeleton was unearthed, and beside it lay a golden cup.

# The Restless Souls of Whitby Abbey

If the legends are true, the majestic ruins of Whitby Abbey in northern Yorkshire, England, are alive with ghosts. First established in A.D. 657 on a cliff overlooking the sea, the abbey was destroyed by the Vikings some two hundred years later, then rebuilt upon the same site by the conquering Normans in 1067. The founder of the original abbey, Saint Hilda, never left, it is said: Her ghost, wrapped in a shroud, frequently appears in one of the abbey's highest windows.

Saint Hilda may also be responsible for another apparition reportedly seen at the abbey. She became well known during her tenure as abbess for ridding the district of snakes. She would drive the snakes to the cliff's edge and decapitate them with her whip. Since then, a great hearselike coach, guided by a headless driver and pulled by four headless horses, has been seen racing along the cliff near the abbey, then plunging over the edge and into the sea.

Perhaps the most troubled ghost of all those said to inhabit the abbey ruins is that of Constance de Beverley, a young nun who broke her sacred vows for the love of a brave but false knight named Marmion. As punishment for her misdeeds, she was bricked up alive in a dungeon in Whitby Abbey. Her ghost has allegedly been seen on the winding stairway leading from the dungeon, cowering and begging release.

# CHAPTER 1

# Phantoms Wrought by Crisis

t dusk one day in the middle of the nineteenth century, a woman and her son sat peacefully in the garden at the back of their house in Clapham, England. Nothing in their surroundings carried any suggestion of the unusual. The hour was pleasant and serene, the fading light throwing long shadows across a rolling lawn that stretched from the house to a wall and gate. Yet in a moment the lives of their family would be transformed by what they believed to be a phantom encounter.

As the two of them sat talking, the son, whose name was John, shifted suddenly in his chair and pointed at something across the lawn. "Mother," he exclaimed, "there's Ellen!"

His surprise was understandable. Ellen, the older of the family's two daughters, had been sent away to Brighton in the south of England by her parents, in hopes of dampening the ardor of an unacceptable romance. Although the girl had been desperately unhappy away from home and suitor, Ellen's mother realized that her husband would be angry over their daughter's early return against his wishes.

"John," she said to her son, "go quickly and tell Ellen to come into the house. Don't say anything to your father."

The young man started to rise from his chair, but sank down again after trying to put his weight on an ankle sprained earlier that day. "I can't run after her," he said. "You'll have to send Mary."

The mother summoned her other daughter from the house and told her to go fetch her sister. "Father shall not know anything about her coming back," the mother instructed. "We'll send her away again in the morning." Mary, a young and energetic girl, ran across the lawn and through the garden gate. She hailed Ellen and was puzzled when her sister failed to respond. She called out again. Wordlessly, Ellen turned down a path that led away from the house, her dark blue cloak billowing behind her.

Mary ran in pursuit, following the path across the softly rolling countryside. At last she caught up and reached out to grasp her sister's arm. "Ellen," she said, "where are you going? Why are you—"

The words caught in her throat. She found that she was unable to take hold of her sister's arm. Her hand seemed to pass directly through the flesh and bone; she felt nothing. A terrible chill ran through her as she watched Ellen turn silently away again and recede.

Numb, the girl walked back to the garden where her mother and brother sat waiting. She told them what had happened. The mother, by now ashen, ran to her husband and repeated the story to him. He shared her conviction that some calamity had befallen their elder daughter.

The next day, their worst fears were confirmed. The previous evening, at the very hour her image had appeared at the house in Clapham, their distraught daughter had thrown herself into the sea and drowned.

Throughout history, from one end of the earth to the other, people have reported seeing apparitions, ghosts, and phantoms. Many accounts of such sightings eventually took the form of folktales. And those tales, often broadly embellished, fostered a popular impression of terrifying specters wafting like smoke through countryside and town, infecting the very atmosphere.

Often enough, an aura of evil or grim vengeance seemed to surround these phantoms. They were envisioned as chain-rattling night creatures implacably bent on redressing some injustice committed during their lifetime. That was the stuff with which to scare small children—and raise more than a few adult hairs in the bargain. It was all hair-raising, to be sure. The question of truth, however, was rarely probed deeply.

Yet that question has always hovered close to the edge of the tales. Do these apparitions have some basis in reality? Does their undubitable power as entertainment conceal more fundamental powers—forces that still lie beyond human understanding, mechanisms still to be defined? In the late nineteenth century, students of the paranormal began to collect and analyze reports of thousands of sightings and visitations. It was their conviction that apparitional appearances deserved serious investigation. One of these researchers, Frederic W. H. Myers, wrote: "Whatever else a 'ghost' may be, it is probably one of the most complex phenomena in nature." That sentiment is still widely shared, and the process of gathering a body of evidence continues to this day.

The documentation is highly provocative. A large number of phantom encounters involve some sort of life crisis, most frequently the ultimate crisis of death. Quite often, the apparition seemingly makes itself known at the very moment or within a few hours of death, as claimed by the family residing in Clapham. And as with that family, the viewers, or percipients, often knew and loved the departed. In many other cases, apparitions have reportedly returned—sometimes years after death—to deliver messages to the living, to honor death compacts made in life, to seek justice, or merely to reassure loved ones that all is well in the world beyond the grave.

Yet phantom appearances seem not to be the province only of the dead. Frequently, apparitions of the living have been said to manifest themselves for no particular reason and with no particular intent; people have seen their doubles, or doppelgängers, separated from the body and performing mundane tasks, entirely oblivious to the observer—or observers, for such spontaneous phantoms have on occasion been witnessed by groups of people.

And then there are the rarest of all phantom encounters, the hauntings, so designated because a specter seems to inhabit a building or locale, revealing itself over time to percipients who did not have any connection with the apparition during life. Hospitals, museums, mansions, and houses of all sorts, dilapidated or not, have been the supposed abodes of ghosts, which may take the form of humans or animals—or indeed may appear in any physical form at all, including that of long-sunken submarines or spectral armies fighting ancient battles.

It is easy, of course, to scoff at reports of encounters with apparitions. Disbelievers hold that if no case is supported by absolutely perfect evidence, then every case should be assumed to have a normal explanation; the sum of any number of zeroes, the skeptics hasten to remind us, remains at zero. The contrary view is that although each

case may be imperfect, the sum of the evidence is cumulative; a single bit of thatch may be weak, but many together can make a sturdy roof.

Moreover, argue the proponents, advances in modern physics may provide an intellectual framework within which such things will be understood. Writes Dr. Christopher Pedler, a noted British physiologist and science fiction writer: "The real trouble is that people won't believe in anything they can't explain. The old rules of physics—where God winds up the system to let it run like clockwork—may produce new technical advances. But they just can't contain the new discoveries. Ghosts, for instance, may be like a footprint which some event has left imprinted in time."

Whatever the explanations may be, the investigators believe that they are gaining ground. As the well-known parapsychologist Louisa Rhine put it in 1981: "Parapsychology is the Cinderella of the sciences. The stepmother, Science, has never favored her. She got a late start and the big sisters like physics, chemistry and biology almost cold-shouldered her out of recognition. It remains to be seen if any fairy prince will rescue her."

There was no Prince Charming and scant encouragement anywhere in 1882, when England's Frederic Myers and a handful of colleagues organized the Society for Psychical Research in order to investigate apparitional experiences. The founding members, however, boasted impressive credentials. Myers was a well-known poet, essayist, and classical lecturer at Trinity College, Cambridge. Joining him were Edmund Gurney, also a classical scholar at Cambridge; Henry Sidgwick, professor of moral philosophy at Cambridge; the tireless researcher Frank Podmore; and a number of other prominent academics, including Sir Oliver Lodge, an eminent physicist at Liverpool University, and Sir William Barrett, who was a professor of physics at the University College of Dublin.

The SPR's founders brought a healthy caution to their investigations. As the society's first official report stated: "The very last thing we expect to produce is a collection of narratives of a startling or blood-chilling character; our pages are far more likely to provoke sleep in the course of perusal than to banish it afterwards."

Still, the Society for Psychical Research attracted enormous public criticism and no little ridicule at the outset. Professor Sidgwick, the society's first president, later recalled being approached by indignant people who "did not like to see so many superior persons spending a serious part of their time on such matters, instead of writing a commentary on Plato, or studying the habits of beetles, or in some other way making a really useful contribution to science or learning."

Even those inclined to be liberal were put off by the franchise the society had outlined for itself. Wrote Sidgwick: "Some not unfriendly critics have given us to understand that if we had only confined ourselves to thought-reading and perhaps clairvoyance and similar phenomena of the mesmeric trance, we might have had countenance; but that by taking in haunted houses and spirit-rapping and so forth, we make ourselves too absurd."

Undaunted, the society's founders were at work in earnest by the close of 1882. One of their first endeavors was to establish a committee to "make a careful investigation of any reports, resting on strong testimony, regarding apparitions at the moment of death." Another committee was entrusted with collecting existing material bearing on the history of psychical matters. "Our somewhat persistent and probing method of inquiry," noted Gurney, "has usually repelled the sentimental or crazy wonder-mongers who hang about the outskirts of such a subject as this."

The society started out by writing letters to London and provincial journals as well as to friends and colleagues requesting any information they might have on apparitional encounters. There was no lack of response; the problem was one of seeking to authenticate the reports, most of which were, at best, anecdotal recollections of past events. The investigators took as a given that human testimony is nothing if not fallible; observations may be incorrect, details sketchy, judgments biased—even when people are genuine-

***In a classic phantom encounter reported in the mid-1800s, a girl in Clapham, England, reached out to touch her older sister when she unexpectedly appeared. The girl's hand met emptiness. She believed that she had seen an apparition, for on the same evening her distraught older sister had committed suicide hundreds of miles away.***

*Considered by many to be the first serious psychical researcher, the Reverend Joseph Glanvill, chaplain to King Charles II, collected many reports of psychic phenomena and, in 1662, personally investigated the reported haunting of a magistrate's home. Glanvill published the results of his research in 1681 under the title Saducismus Triumphatus; the book's opening engraving depicts some of the cases related within.*

ly trying to relate the truth. The researchers applied rigorous standards to each case; whenever possible, they personally interviewed the narrator and sought out other living persons involved in the matter in order to get independent corroboration of the story.

It did not take the Society for Psychical Research investigators long to become convinced that they were on to something. As expressed in the society's first report: "The point in the evidence that impresses us is not its exciting or terrific quality, but its overwhelming quantity—overwhelming, we mean, to any further doubting of the reality of the class of phenomena."

Some of the cases were stunning, among them two experiences in which the percipients were unquestionably in full possession of their senses and highly unlikely to fall victim to delusions or visions. In the first incident, a Mr. Rawlinson was getting dressed in his home in Cheltenham one morning in December 1881 when he felt a powerful presence in the room. "On looking around," he related, "I saw no one, but then instantaneously (in my mind's eye, I suppose), every feature of the face and form of my old friend, X, arose. This, as you may imagine, made a great impression on me, and I went at once into my wife's room and told her what had occurred, at the same time stating that I feared Mr. X must be dead."

Rawlinson and his wife spoke of it with growing concern several times that day. The next day, Rawlinson received a letter from X's brother reporting that X had died at a quarter to nine the previous morning. Recounted Rawlinson: "This was the very time the occurrence happened in my dressing room." Rawlinson felt compelled to note that "we had heard some two months previously that X was suffering from cancer, but still we were in no immediate apprehension of his death." And he added: "I never on any other occasion had any hallucination of the senses, and sincerely trust I never again shall."

The other case was even more remarkable. The event had taken place on September 8, 1855, and it involved G. F. Russell Colt, later a British Army captain, but at the time a schoolboy at home with his parents near Edinburgh, Scotland. The family was a military one, and the eldest son, Oliver, age nineteen, was serving as a lieutenant with the Seventh Royal Fusiliers at Sebastopol in the Crimean War. Waking one night, Russell found his brother Oliver in his room; the youth seemed to be kneeling and was enveloped in a bright, phosphorescent mist.

Russell told himself that his eyes were playing tricks on him; what he was seeing was nothing more than a beam of moonlight playing on a towel draped over a chair. The apparition persisted, however, "looking lovingly, imploringly and sadly at me," said Russell. It seemed so real that the schoolboy leaped from his bed and went to the window. But there was no moonlight; the night was black and heavy with rain. By now thoroughly frightened, Russell fled from the room. Looking behind him, he saw that the apparition had a terrible wound on the right temple from which blood was gushing forth.

When Russell told his father, the older man snorted and advised him "not to repeat such nonsense." Yet it was anything but nonsense. More than a fortnight after the incident occurred, the family received the news of Oliver's death; he had been killed in the storming of a Turkish redoubt. Sometime after, they learned that a bullet had struck Oliver in the right temple, precisely where the wound had appeared to Russell. And there was more. Related Russell: "Oliver had then been some months before Sebastopol and had recently written to me in low spirits and evidently unwell, a letter to which I replied urging him to cheer up, adding half-facetiously, that if anything did happen to him, he must let me see him again in the old room where we had so often had . . . a cozy chat at night."

In 1886, Gurney, Myers, and Podmore published what was the most ambitious piece of psychical research to date, a two-volume, 1,400-page survey entitled *Phantasms of the Living.* The purpose of the report, wrote Myers, was "to open an inquiry which was manifestly impending, and to lay the foundation-stone of a study which will loom large in the approaching age." The sheer size of the work indicated the massive volume of evidence and firsthand accounts available to the psychical researchers, and the authors believed that the book banished any remaining doubts about the reality of phantom encounters. The goal, then, was to attempt to classify and understand these experiences. In so doing, the three investigators opened a debate that continues to this day.

In attempting to explain apparitions, *Phantasms of the Living* advanced a theory based on telepathy—a term actually coined by Myers to replace the unwieldy "thought-transference." In the cases collected in *Phantasms,* the authors said, they examined "the ability of one mind to impress or be impressed by another mind other than through the recognized channels of sense." In other words, the percipient might actually be receiving a telepathic signal from the apparent—the person represented by the apparition. In fact, according to this theory of telepathy, the apparent need not be present in any sense in order to be represented as a phantom. As Myers later summed it up: "Instead of describing a 'ghost' as a dead person permitted to communicate with the living, let us define it as a *manifestation of persistent personal energy.*"

Although this theory proved instantly controversial, there appeared to be much in favor of it. Of the 701 cases discussed in *Phantasms of the Living,* more than half concerned reports of phantom appearances or other impressions in which the manifestation coincided with either the death of the apparent or some other critical moment in that person's life. "On reviewing the evidence thus obtained," wrote Edmund Gurney, "we were struck with the great predominance of alleged apparitions at or near the moment of death. And a new light seemed to be thrown on these phenomena by the unexpected frequency of accounts of apparitions of living persons, coincident with moments of danger or crisis." To these cases, the SPR applied the term "crisis apparitions," suggesting that in such moments of crisis, telepathic communications seem more likely to take place.

*Phantasms of the Living* proved to be only the first step in a master plan of the society—the "foundation-stone," as Myers had termed it. The next phase, which was pursued over a period of five years, was an exhaustive *Census of Hallucinations,* undertaken with characteristic thoroughness by Professor Sidgwick.

Sidgwick hoped to discover what percentage of the general population had experienced hallucinations that might be considered apparitional. Toward that end, he carefully developed a census question that would encompass three types of hallucinations—those of sight, hearing, and touch—while excluding dream experiences. The question read: "Have you ever, when believing yourself to be completely awake, had a vivid impression of seeing or being touched by a living being or inanimate object, or of hearing a voice; which impression, so far as you could discover, was not due to any external physical cause?"

The question was printed on a form that required the person being canvassed to state only yes or no and to give name, address, and occupation. Those answering yes were provided with another form on which they were asked to put down the details. Forms were circulated by 410 volunteer census collectors and drew an astounding 17,000 responses. The survey was an international one, with replies coming from Austria, Brazil, France, Germany, Italy, and Russia, along with those of Great Britain.

The results defied all expectations. Nearly 10 percent of those polled—1,684 persons—admitted to having experienced sensory hallucinations of the kind described in the census question. The group was made up of 1,029 women and 655 men. Of the total cases reported, 1,087 were visual and 493 auditory, whereas 2 had involved the sense of touch; 129 of the phantom encounters had been experienced by more than one person.

For purposes of his investigation, Sidgwick defined crisis apparitions according to an arbitrary "margin of coincidence." In effect, he contended, a phantom sighted within a period of twelve hours either before or after a crisis in the apparent's life could reasonably be called a crisis appari-

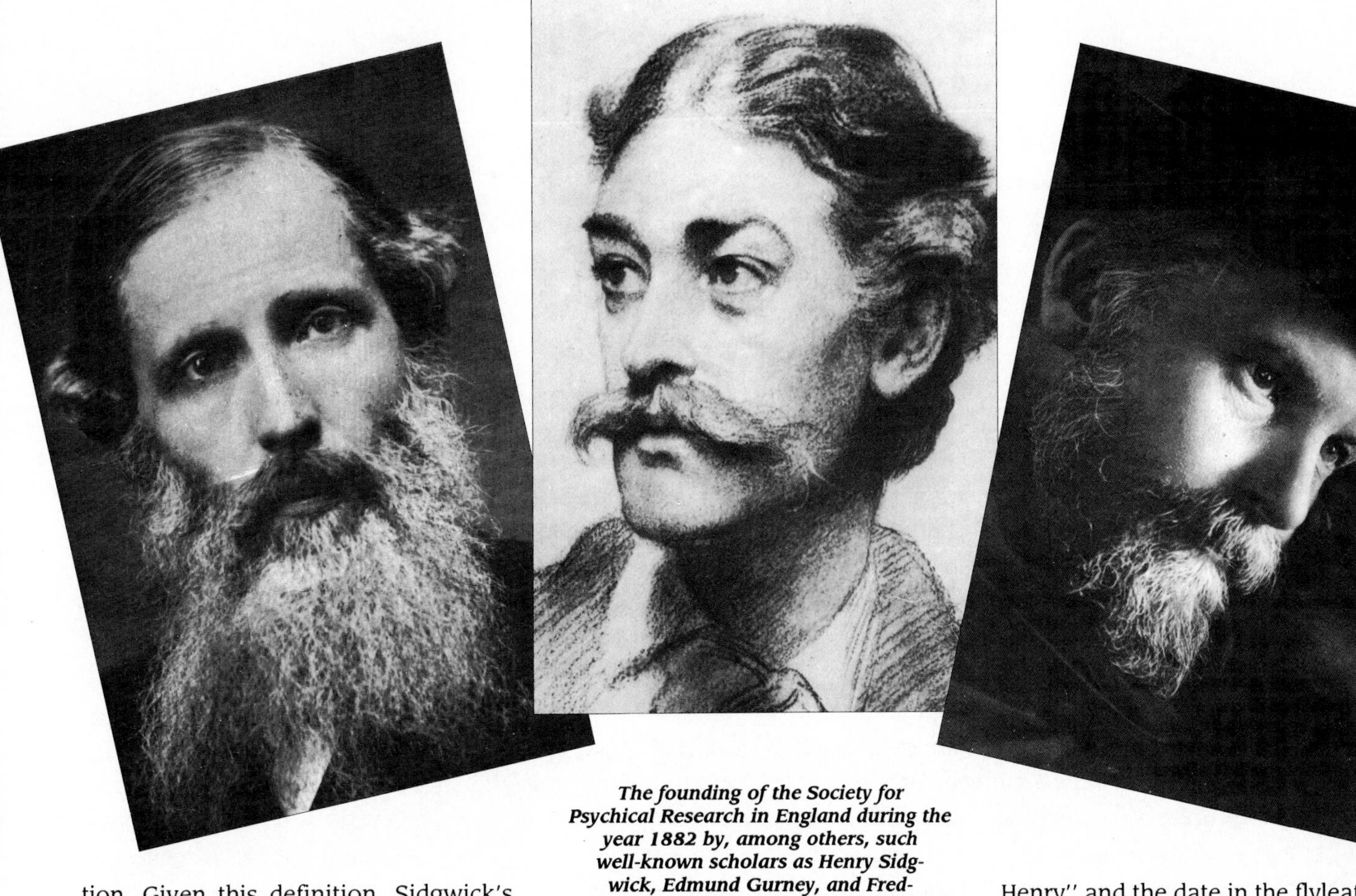

***The founding of the Society for Psychical Research in England during the year 1882 by, among others, such well-known scholars as Henry Sidgwick, Edmund Gurney, and Frederic Myers (left to right) lent an aura of respectability to the study and investigation of paranormal experiences.***

tion. Given this definition, Sidgwick's data indicated that such apparitions occurred with far greater regularity than any other type of apparitional experience. As a matter of fact, the likelihood of an apparition appearing coincident with a crisis in the apparent's life proved 440 times greater than the chances of one appearing for any other discernible reason.

The accounts of apparitional experiences collected in both *Phantasms of the Living* and the *Census of Hallucinations* shared a number of features. A typical case was that of Mrs. Sabine Baring-Gould of Exeter, England. On January 3, 1840, Mrs. Baring-Gould sat at her dining room table reading the Bible by the light of a candle. Looking up, she reported afterward, she saw her brother, Henry, sitting at the other side of the table. The scene appeared entirely natural—except for the fact that Henry was at that time serving aboard a Royal Navy ship in the South Atlantic.

Although agitated, Mrs. Baring-Gould refused to panic, perhaps calmed by the kindly expression she saw on her brother's face. Neither one spoke, but the woman stared steadily at her brother for several moments, until his form grew dim and faded away before her eyes. Realizing what this might mean, Mrs. Baring-Gould jotted the words "Saw Henry" and the date in the flyleaf of her Bible. A month later, word came that her brother had died at sea—his death had occurred at the very moment his sister saw his figure sitting across from her.

Unfortunately, there were no witnesses to the appearance of Mrs. Baring-Gould's brother. Moreover, the woman did not tell anyone of the experience until after his death became widely known.

The case of Mrs. Anne Collyer of Camden, New Jersey, although similar in many respects to Mrs. Baring-Gould's, provided a crucial element of third-party confirmation. On the night of January 3, 1856, Mrs. Collyer awoke to find her son Joseph standing in the doorway of her bedroom, staring intently at her. As in the case of Mrs. Baring-Gould, the appearance of Mrs. Collyer's son was decidedly impossible, since he was at that time in command of a steamboat on the Mississippi River, more than 1,000 miles to the west. Shocked enough to see her son so unexpectedly, Mrs. Collyer was even more disturbed to note that his face and head were terribly disfigured and wrapped in a crude bandage. He wore a dirty white nightshirt, which she did not recognize, although she later described it as looking something like a surplice.

The next morning, Mrs. Collyer related to her husband and four daughters what she had seen. Her family gave the story little credit, believing that she had simply experienced a very bad dream.

Mrs. Collyer knew better, but it was almost two weeks before the news that she dreaded finally arrived: Captain Collyer had been killed in a steamboat collision. Part of the ship's mast had fallen on him, splitting his skull. His death had occurred at almost the precise moment that his mother had seen his apparition.

The case proved of particular interest to the Society for Psychical Research because of the independent testimony provided by Mrs. Collyer's husband and daughters. All attested to the truth of her story, which she had told in detail well before her son's death became known through more conventional channels. Another of Mrs. Collyer's sons added a further detail after viewing the body: Captain Collyer, roused from his cabin in the middle of the night, had been wearing a white nightshirt, which became soiled in the collision. At the time of his death, he had been attired exactly as his mother saw him.

Not all crisis apparition cases involve intimate family members. In a more recent case that took place in New Delhi, India, a phantom appears to have manifested itself to the wrong person, even though a more likely percipient—the apparent's granddaughter—was present in the same room. These unusual instances are known to researchers as "bystander cases."

In April of 1968, Dr. Bhanu Iyengar, a college professor, was in the hospital recovering from a difficult childbirth. Though Dr. Iyengar's condition was not critical, she had developed a prolonged high fever and slipped in and out of consciousness for several days. Her friend Suman Kirti often visited during this period, sitting quietly at her bedside along with Dr. Iyengar's mother.

One afternoon, drowsy and half asleep, Dr. Iyengar opened her eyes and saw Miss Kirti's grandfather, whom she had met on one or two occasions. The old man stood at the foot of her bed with a strangely plaintive look on his face. Leaning forward, he said, "Would you not send my child home?" Dr. Iyengar assumed that her high fever had brought on hallucinations and quickly rolled over to the other side of the hospital bed, expecting that the image would vanish. It did not, however. The old man again appeared before her and repeated the same words, "Would you not send my child home?"

The feverish woman was growing excited now, but she saw by the calm expressions on the faces of the two women at her bedside that they had not seen the apparition. Frantically, Dr. Iyengar urged Miss Kirti to go home to her grandfather at once. The young woman, thinking her friend had become delirious, assured the upset Dr. Iyengar that her grandfather was fine. As a matter of fact, he was due to pick her up at the hospital within the hour. Dr. Iyengar was not mollified. Though she did not talk about what she had seen, the woman continued with rising hysteria to urge her friend to go home. Finally, a skeptical Miss Kirti agreed to make a telephone call to her grandfather. At once her skepticism turned to shock and grief: Her grandfather had passed away just ten minutes before.

This episode is seen by psychic investigators as suggestive on a number of levels. Although the two people in the hospital room who did not see the apparition provide independent verification that Dr. Iyengar had an unusual experience, the crucial question remains: Why did the supposed phantom not appear directly to Miss Kirti? Perhaps, some psychical researchers have theorized, Dr. Iyengar's fever caused her to be in a state that was particularly receptive to hallucinations.

An even more remarkable case of bystander apparition had been reported in America nearly 150 years earlier on board a sailing vessel voyaging from Maryland to the West Indies. In this instance, the phantom not only manifested itself to a pair of complete strangers but continued to be seen repeatedly throughout what became a desperate trip, always foretelling some danger.

The incidents began just before the vessel set sail from

the port of Annapolis. During the night watch, one of the sailors started calling insistently for the captain to come on deck. When the skipper finally appeared, the man told him that a woman in black had inquired after him and had then disappeared. A search of the entire vessel was made, but they could not discover any sign of the mysterious visitor. Thinking that the sailor was drunk, as was all too often the case, the captain issued a sharp reprimand to him and retired to his cabin.

Again, at about 2:00 A.M., the captain was roused by a call from the deck. The woman in black had shown herself to another sailor, this one the soul of sobriety. But once more, no sign of the wraithlike visitor could be found. By now, the superstitious seamen were clamoring to flee the ship, even offering their advance wages, so sure were they that a curse of doom had been leveled at the vessel. But the master shrugged off their entreaties and set sail next morning for southern waters.

When they were two days out on the open sea, a terrible storm blew up, with deafening thunderclaps and winds so fierce that before long the ship was running under only her main and fore-topmast stay sails. Between the hours of six and eight o'clock at night, the two sailors claimed that the supernatural being again appeared before them. As she did, the gale increased in fury, and the seas swelled to mountainous heights.

Precisely at midnight, the woman in black appeared yet a fourth time. And now the winds reached hurricane velocity, churning the sea to a froth and threatening to hurl the vessel on her beam ends. For four hours, the banshee winds ripped and tore; not a shred of canvas remained aloft; the ship's boats were smashed or carried away and much of the deckhouse was in ruins. Finally, at 4:00 A.M., the wild storm suddenly died; the wind abated, the seas moderated, and the moon came out.

Nothing untoward occurred during the remainder of the voyage south. But when the vessel was in Guadeloupe taking on a cargo of sugar, the phantom woman in black appeared for a fifth time; the visitation was followed two days later by an outbreak of yellow fever that claimed the life of one of the crew.

When the battered vessel finally returned to her home port of Baltimore, a letter awaited the captain. His wife, who resided on Nantucket, was dead. She had passed away at almost exactly the moment when the woman in black first appeared before the sailor on watch in Annapolis.

An equally intriguing case, taken from the journals of the SPR, was that of Captain Eldred Bowyer-Bower, a British airman who was shot down and killed over France during World War I. At the moment of his death, his phantom was reportedly sighted by two people, both relatives, many thousands of miles apart, one of whom was in India and the other in England.

On the morning of March 19, 1917, Captain Bowyer-Bower's half-sister, Mrs. Spearman, sat cradling her baby in a hotel room in Calcutta, when she turned to see the flier standing behind her. His face, she later reported, wore a "dear mischievous look," as if his appearance was part of some youthful prank. Although the captain's presence in her room was unexpected, Mrs. Spearman was delighted to see him, having no indication that anything had gone wrong. With a brief word of greeting, she turned to put her baby into its crib so that she and Captain Bowyer-Bower could have a talk. When she turned around again, extending her arms to give her half-brother a hug of welcome, he had disappeared.

At nearly the same moment, halfway around the world in Great Britain, Captain Bowyer-Bower's sister, called Mrs. Chater, had a similarly unsettling experience. As Mrs. Chater was dressing early in the morning, her three-year-old daughter came skipping gaily into the bedroom to report that downstairs she had just seen "Uncle Alley Boy," a nickname the young girl had for Captain Bowyer-Bower. When Mrs. Chater reminded her daughter that her Uncle Eldred was in France, the child stubbornly repeated that she had seen him downstairs.

Later that same day, Mrs. Chater wrote of the incident

# Mr. Tweedie's Ghostly Gossip

The nineteenth century was the heyday of ghosts in England. Caught in a conflict between science and religion, between reason and sentimentality, Victorian society developed a romantic obsession with—and morbid curiosity about—death and spirits of the dead. This obsession was reflected in the popular ghost stories of the day and even spilled into other areas of entertainment. Eager to capitalize, an astute businessman named George R. Tweedie conceived "Gossip about Ghosts," a lecture illustrated with lantern slides detailing fifty stories of ghosts and the supernatural.

Tweedie, a former instructor at the Royal Polytechnic Institution in London, drew quite a crowd, as evidenced by a review in the *Pall Mall Gazette* on September 23, 1891. "Lectures on Ghosts and Witches," the newspaper wrote, "are getting in demand," and Tweedie's collection of illustrations "shows that Ghostlore is more refined than it used to be."

Tweedie's presentation, which cost each patron a sixpence to attend, contained no objective analysis of the phenomenon of apparitional encounters; he merely offered an entertaining look at some ghost stories of recent history. At the end of his address, however, he revealed his personal feelings about what he termed "this somewhat grim chapter in the history of human nature." Said Tweedie: "My own opinion is that the inscrutable workings of mind, conscience, imagination, or whatever it may be called, are the real exciting cause of the vast majority of apparitions. . . . The average healthy man, properly educated, temperate in all things, goes through the world untroubled by any such phantasms as we have seen tonight." A representative sampling of those alleged phantasms appears on these pages.

***A Bavarian man was reportedly visited by the ghost of his wife, the victim of his unruly temper. At his remorseful promise to control his anger, the wife's apparition decided to stay. But when the man later flew into a rage, the ghost vanished, leaving only her empty, hooded cloak.***

***In 1647, a ship laden with riches and carrying numerous passengers supposedly vanished on a voyage from America to England. The ship was never found, but months later witnesses claimed to have seen, at the ship's port of origin, a spectral vessel aloft in a cloud.***

*This illustration depicts a case concerning a servant girl who was taken ill at the home of her employers. Word was sent to the girl's family in a distant town, but on the final evening of her life, no one had yet arrived. Late that night, however, as the girl breathed her last, the figure of an elderly woman appeared in the room. According to the attending maid, the woman gazed at the form in the bed, then vanished. The next day the dead girl's mother arrived, and the maid recognized her as the visitor she had seen—in phantom form—the night before.*

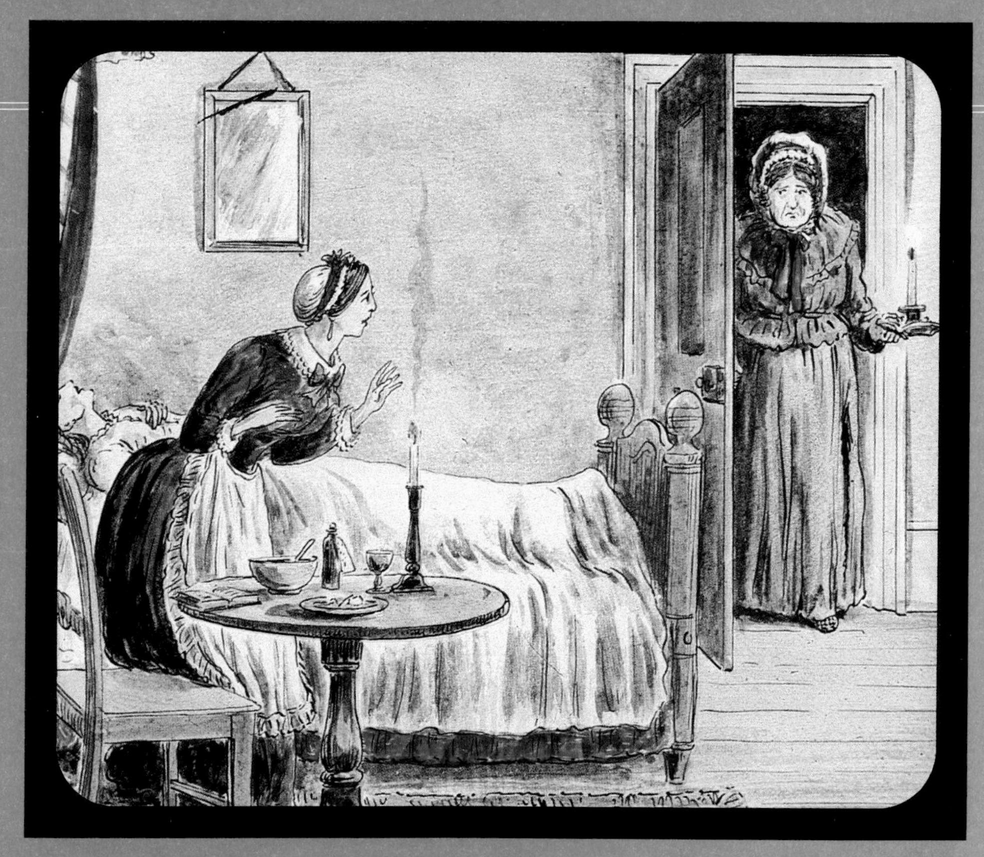

*The grisly tale behind this illustration involves the death of one Hamilton Tighe, murdered by a sailor at the bidding of his ship's captain and Tighe's devious stepmother. Afterward, the guilty conspirators were mercilessly haunted by the headless man's apparition.*

*In this seventeenth-century woodcut, the ghost of Sir George Villiers, father of the Duke of Buckingham, visits a king's officer with information to save the duke from an untimely death. The officer delivered the message, but the duke was found murdered a few months later.*

in a letter to her mother—not because she found the occurrence so remarkable but to illustrate the fact that the girl thought of her uncle frequently. Neither Mrs. Chater nor Mrs. Spearman learned of Captain Bowyer-Bower's death for several more days.

The records of the Society for Psychical Research hold yet another dramatic incident concerning a World War I British aviator, this one reported by Lieutenant J. J. Larkin. On December 7, 1918, less than a month after the armistice, Lieutenant Larkin sat writing letters in his quarters when a good friend, Lieutenant David E. McConnel, walked into the room. Wearing his flying gear, McConnel announced his intention of taking a Sopwith Camel biplane out for machine-gun practice. McConnel, a rakish young pilot who made a point of wearing a navy cap with his uniform, remarked to his friend: "I expect to be back in time for tea." Then the young flier headed off for the airfield. A moment later McConnel returned to retrieve a map he had forgotten, and then was off again.

Larkin thought no more of the incident until sometime between 3:15 and 3:30 in the afternoon, when McConnel burst into the room with a cheery word of greeting.

"Back already?" Larkin asked.

"Yes," McConnel replied. "Got there all right, had a good trip. Well, so long!"

With these words, McConnel slipped out of the room.

At 3:45, a senior officer entered the room and said, "I hope McConnel gets back soon."

"He is back," Larkin said. "He was here a few minutes ago." Unfortunately, Larkin was unable to locate his friend then or ever. Within the hour, he came across a group of fellow officers discussing a fatal airplane crash that had happened earlier that afternoon. Slowly, Larkin realized that the dead pilot was none other than McConnel, whose death, according to all evidence, had occurred at just past three o'clock that afternoon, the same time that Larkin had been speaking to him.

The incident, which was corroborated by the senior officer, is remarkable in that it was auditory as well as visual—Lieutenant Larkin apparently heard and spoke to McConnel in a manner so lifelike that he did not realize he had spoken to an apparition until he later found out about the death of his friend.

Indeed, most phantom encounters involve apparents whose habits and appearance are extremely familiar to the percipient. Consequently, some skeptics contend that many so-called apparitional experiences are really just the products of overheated imaginations—and no doubt that is sometimes the truth of the matter. A report of an encounter such as Lieutenant Larkin's, for instance, lies open to the charge that the pilot merely imagined the familiar presence of his friend, despite the young officer's convictions to the contrary. In most instances, there is no way of obtaining foolproof evidence of the validity of an apparitional experience, and this inability remains a key stumbling block for psychical research.

Yet a number of cases resist much of the criticism leveled at such studies. Percipients seem to know certain exact details—the head wound suffered by Lieutenant Colt in the Crimea, the soiled nightshirt worn by riverboat captain Collyer—that many researchers maintain could not possibly be acquired except through the agency of a genuine apparition. One such case was the famed "Full Court Dress" incident, which occurred sometime in the 1830s or 1840s and was reported years afterward to the SPR.

The percipient was an Englishwoman who awoke to the sound of loud knocking at two o'clock one morning. Going over to the window, she discovered her mother, from whom she had been estranged for a number of years, standing at the doorstep. At once the woman roused her husband, but when he went to the window he saw nothing. The woman was not only convinced that it had been her mother on the doorstep, but she described in detail her mother's "full Court dress," a gown appropriate for wearing at a royal function.

Later the next day, the woman heard news of her mother, the first she had received in many years. Her moth-

***Some inanimate objects, such as an heirloom clock (right) that belonged to Helen Verba of Denver, Colorado, are said to convey the message of a loved one's death. In Verba's case, the clock was said to have stopped working on at least three separate occasions at the exact moment a family member died. The dial of the clock reportedly turned upside down after Verba put it up for sale at an antique shop.***

er had indeed been at a royal ball at Kensington Palace the previous evening, but had become ill suddenly and been rushed home—where she died at 2:00 A.M., still wearing her full Court dress.

These cases as well as the numerous others that have been collected and analyzed by the Society for Psychical Research sparked a lively and prolonged debate about the nature and substance of apparitions. One of the central points of contention—and one that is still discussed to this day—is the question of whether apparitions are physical or nonphysical. In other words, do phantoms occupy actual space or are they purely subjective hallucinations that exist only in the mind of the percipient?

Like his colleague Frederic Myers, Edmund Gurney believed in apparitions as subjective phenomena, unique to the percipient, that could be explained only in relation to telepathy. In his opinion, the apparent is not actually present in any sense at the scene of the phantom encounter. Rather, he proposed that the percipient receives a telepathic cue from the apparent, a cue often caused by a crisis or near-death experience, which the percipient then utilizes to project an apparition.

A flaw in Gurney's theory was that it did not adequately account for the occasional occurrence of "collective phenomena," or apparitions seen by more than one person at the same time. Gurney attempted to explain these rare events by introducing the idea of "contagious telepathy," in which an apparition projected by one person might infect the minds of others so that they too see the same figure. The theory, however, was not a very convincing one, and even Gurney himself did not seem to be entirely comfortable with it.

Myers put forward a revised theory that attempted to overcome the limitations of Gurney's hypothesis. Although Myers agreed that phantoms were not physical manifestations in the strictest sense, he did contend that they occupied a physical space that he called "metetherial," a sort of fourth-dimensional field that intertwines with our own physical space. In Myers's view, this explained why some apparitions might appear to have a combination of both physical and nonphysical qualities.

The beliefs of Edmund Gurney and Frederick Myers exerted a considerable influence on the psychical researchers who followed them, including G. N. M. Tyrrell, who became president of the Society for Psychical Research in 1945. Tyrrell devoted forty years of his life to the study of apparitions, although, like his predecessors, he had a strong grounding in the physical sciences, holding a degree in physics and mathematics from London University. Throughout his long tenure with the society, Tyrrell attempted to revise and reconsider the existing apparitional theories.

In his book *Apparitions,* which drew on the early cases collected by the SPR, Tyrrell broke down all apparitional incidents into the four broad categories that are still generally recognized: apparitions of the living, crisis apparitions, postmortem apparitions, and continual, or recurring, apparitions. He then went on to postulate the existence of layers of unconscious creative potential in the minds of apparition percipients, to which he gave the rather whimsically theatrical names of "producer" and "stage carpenter." These creative elements, Tyrrell theorized, teamed up with those of the apparent to produce a joint "apparitional drama," which Tyrrell described as "not a physical phenomenon but a sensory hallucination." Any flaws in the production, such as the wrong clothing or a mixed-up setting, Tyrrell airily dismissed as nothing more than faulty stagecraft.

Nevertheless, Tyrrell's hypotheses did address many of the difficulties of the earlier theories. Some of the hard-to-explain aspects of certain apparitional experiences could be understood as the "stagecraft" of the apparitional drama. If, for example, an apparition appeared to open a door, the door did not physically open. The idea of the door opening seemed dramatically appropriate, so movement took place in a hallucination—which he interpreted as evidence of an efficient "stage carpenter."

But no single theory, however detailed, has managed to adequately explain each of the hundreds of apparitional cases examined by the society. Tyrrell's views of a subtle creative apparatus at work in both the percipient and the apparent, for example, does not seem to account for several instances of apparitional appearances by dogs, cats, and horses. Sir Henry Rider Haggard, the English novelist, reported in July 1904 a vivid crisis apparition of his daughter's prized retriever. The writer saw the dog lying motionless in a bed of reeds; it turned out that the animal had, in fact, fallen from a bridge to its death in a marshy stream.

On an even more creative level, a phantom animal was not seen but only heard. In this case, a Mr. and Mrs. Beauchamp owned a little mongrel dog humorously named Megatherium, after a species of large sloth. One night the Beauchamps were awakened to hear the sound of their pet's footsteps in the bedroom. But they could not find the animal and assumed that they had been mistaken about the sounds when they saw that the door to their bedroom was closed. A bit later, the couple was awakened again—now by their daughter pounding on the door and shouting that the dog was dying. The Beauchamps rushed downstairs to find Megatherium entangled and strangling in his collar, from which they swiftly rescued him. Megatherium might have been an intelligent little dog, but this bit of dramaturgy may have been a bit beyond him.

Similarly, the case of Mrs. May Clerke admits of no easy explanation, even when considered in the light of the various theories. In August of 1864, Mrs. Clerke sat reading a book on the terrace of her house on Barbados when a maid approached and asked, "Missus, who was that gentleman talking to you just now?"

Mrs. Clerke replied that she was quite alone and had spoken with no one. But the maid insisted that she had seen a tall, pale young man earnestly speaking to Mrs. Clerke and had thought it odd that her mistress failed to acknowledge him in any way.

In the familiar pattern of crisis apparitions, Mrs. Clerke later discovered that her brother, a tall, pale man, had died after a short illness at just the time that the maid spotted the figure on the terrace. The maid had no apparent predisposition to witness an apparition of Mrs. Clerke's brother. In fact, she had never even met him.

Another perplexing variation in the phenomenon of crisis apparitions involves "death compacts," or agreements made between two living people that the first to die will attempt to contact the survivor. Two remarkable instances of death-compact apparitions are recorded in *Phantasms of the Living*. The first involves Lord Henry Brougham, a prominent figure in English civic life in the early half of the nineteenth century and a Lord High Chancellor of England from 1830 to 1834.

As a young man, Lord Brougham attended Edinburgh University with his closest friend, dubbed G. in the SPR account. There, the two friends fell into frequent conversation about survival of death and the immortality of the soul. The possibility that the dead would appear to the living intrigued both men, with the result that the two made a solemn vow that the first to die would make every attempt to appear to the survivor in some form.

The two men went their separate ways after leaving the school, and over the years they lost track of each other. Eventually, Lord Brougham later admitted, he had nearly forgotten the existence of his former friend from the university. Many years later, while traveling through Sweden, he had occasion to recall his friend G. One night, as he lay soaking in a hot bath after a long day of travel, Lord Brougham glanced over at the chair where he had left his clothing and saw the figure of G. The next thing Lord Brougham knew, he lay sprawled on the bathroom floor; the apparition had disappeared.

Only upon returning to Edinburgh did Lord Brougham discover that his friend had died on the same date and at the same time as the strange appearance.

Despite having made the death compact in his youth, Lord Brougham was far from an ideal percipient. Even when confronted with the sight of his old friend, and upon learning about the coincidence of the time of his death, he continued to harbor strong reservations concerning the validity of the experience. Writing in his journal some years later, he referred to the whole thing as a "singular coincidence" and speculated at length on the nature of dreams and coincidences.

Sometimes, however, the percipient of a ghostly visitor seems to be left with physical evidence of the otherworldly encounter. In 1884, for example, a Professor Romanes recorded a curious incident involving a handsome young Englishman named Griffiths, who was about to marry a lovely French girl. Chaperoned by their mothers, the betrothed pair had just spent a pleasant holiday in Italy and the south of France and were on their way home, the Griffiths to London and the French girl with her mother to Paris. On the night before crossing the channel to England, young Griffiths was awakened from a heavy sleep to hear the voice of his fiancée pleading with him in French to come instantly to her in Paris.

Griffiths then saw his betrothed coming toward him and felt her reach out to grasp his arm in her hand. An awful fright took hold of him, and the Englishman rushed to his mother's room. As might be expected, she calmly reassured him that everything was all right, and he returned to his bed. He fell briefly asleep but was soon conscious of an intense pain on his arm. Rolling up his nightshirt sleeve, he found an ugly red spot and a rising blister where his love had touched him.

Next morning, Griffiths visited a doctor, who told him that he had suffered a severe burn. But that seemed impossible—and doubly so because the doctor could not find the slightest indication of fire or corrosive chemical on the sleeve of the nightshirt.

Later that day, a telegram arrived from Paris bringing news of his fiancée's sudden death, following an illness of only a few hours. Some time after, Griffiths learned that as she lay dying she had called out for him in the very words he had heard in his bedroom.

Cases of such vivid physical evidence are virtually unheard of in the recent history of psychical research. For the most part, the traces of an apparitional visit, when there are any at all, are fleeting and usually purely sensory—a familiar aroma of pipe smoke, for example, or the sound of a favorite tune being whistled. But so-called somatic dramas, in which the percipient actually experiences the pain felt by the agent, have been reported.

In an incident recorded by Louisa Rhine, a woman in California awoke at 4:00 A.M. one day in 1955, convinced that she was dying. She had the sensation of blood pouring from her head as if from a wound and found herself gasping and choking. As her husband helped her drink some water, the woman distinctly heard the voice of her son call, "Oh, Mama, help me." Two days later, after a doctor assured her that nothing was physically wrong with her, the woman learned that her son, a soldier stationed in Germany, had received a fatal gunshot wound to the head at exactly the time of her attack. She

# Stylish Selections from the Spectral Wardrobe

The centuries-old popular image of ghosts is one of diaphanous figures hovering in flowing white robes. Loose, pale clothing is indeed said to be favored by ghostly visitors. But according to one nineteenth-century British commentator, "These are chiefly the churchyard ghosts, who have no particular business, but . . . to scare drunken rustics from tumbling over their graves." While white-clad ghosts have been reported in places other than graveyards, many more tales of phantom encounters suggest that colorful clothing must also hang in the spectral closet.

That ghosts are said to appear dressed at all has aroused controversy among both psychical researchers and skeptics. Although ancient civilizations left earthly garments in graves for use in the next life, it is difficult to imagine a ghost pondering which suit of clothes to slip into or, as nineteenth-century English caricaturist George Cruikshank put it, browsing in "spiritual outfitting shops."

Yet reports of naked ghosts are rare. In a well-known Scandinavian story, the scantily clothed figure of a man ostracized by fellow villagers returned after his death to haunt them. And Japanese ghosts are said to appear quite often in clothing that is disheveled and bloody. But propriety prevails in most cases. Apparitions are usually described as being attired as they were in life, and reports of phantoms clad in suits of armor, silken gowns, or monk robes are not unusual.

To explain such costumes, Frank Podmore, an early member of the Society for Psychical Research, suggested that an apparition existed only in the witness's mind and that the percipient would outfit it in a familiar manner. If so, the percipient's mind may not only provide the apparel but also imbue it with a particular significance. In one case, for example, white clothing signified to the percipient the state of the ghost's spiritual progress. As the story goes, the widow of a notorious usurer was praying near her husband's grave when she allegedly saw him nearby wearing a black gown and looking glum. After seven years, she testified, the gown had faded from black to white, and her husband's shade exhibited a cheerful countenance—as if it had achieved redemption beyond the grave.

became convinced that what she had heard had been his death cry, and that the pain she had experienced had been his final agony.

In a similar instance at about the same time, a man preparing to go to work in New York felt himself suddenly stricken with what felt like a blow to the head, leaving him dizzy and somewhat confused for much of the morning. Only later did he learn that his mother in California had simultaneously suffered the same symptoms as the result of a blood clot in the head. After she had recovered, the mother recalled that she had cried out for her son just as the agonizing pain commenced.

These cases, both of which occurred in the United States, illustrate the new directions taken by psychical research in the 1950s. Following World War II, the amount of such work done in Great Britain declined considerably, while the American counterpart of the SPR, the American Society for Psychical Research, flourished.

In 1953, for example, Dr. Hornell Hart, a Duke University sociologist and an active member of the ASPR, undertook a complete reevaluation of the apparitional theories that had been formulated to date. Rejecting earlier notions of telepathic projection, Hart maintained that apparitions possessed a certain amount of independent consciousness, and that they reacted to physical objects and people in their environment just as a normal, living person would. After years of research, Hart came to believe that apparitions represented some sort of "ultraphysical vehicle" that could be liberated from the human body at death and even during life. Hart called this the "soul body."

Dr. Louisa Rhine took a different view. In the course of amassing the largest collection of spontaneous hallucination incidents on record in the United States, Dr. Rhine came to think of apparitions as "psi experiences, or as ESP hallucinations." Her theory of clairvoyance proposed that an apparition is solely created by the percipient, based on clairvoyant impressions of the apparent and his or her situation, whether it be death, physical danger, or any other crisis. Both the Hart and Rhine theories could account for the somatic dramas experienced by the California woman and the New York man.

During the course of her work, Dr. Rhine came across a number of crisis experiences that fell into the category of death visions, or "meeting cases," also known as near-death experiences. In this type of alleged apparitional phenomenon, it is the percipient, not the apparent, who is in crisis. Often a person who is near death seems to see, or calls out to, departed friends or relatives who appear to have hastened to the borderland between life and death in order to extend a welcome. Incidents such as this one are notoriously difficult to authenticate, however, since percipients seldom linger long enough to be interviewed by a trained investigator.

Deathbed apparitions have been recorded in literature and history for centuries, but they were not studied in any scientific detail until the early 1960s, when Dr. Karlis Osis, using the *Census of Hallucinations* as a pattern, surveyed 10,000 nurses and doctors throughout the United States in an attempt to gather information about near-death experiences. Although one psychic likened the process to "catching a butterfly with a bear trap," Dr. Osis's study led him to conclude that the majority of deathbed hallucinations are truly apparitional, rather than the result of a brain disturbed by the processes of dying.

"While some hallucinatory behavior was found to be of pathological origin, just ramblings about this-world concerns," he wrote, "in the greater part of the cases, the visions did not look like ordinary hallucinations. For example, the dying person might be quite rational and well oriented in all respects, but still insist that he or she saw apparitions that were 'coming to take him away' to another world. Generally, such experiences were of shorter duration, more coherent and more related to the situation of dying and of an afterlife than the ramblings of a sick brain."

Despite the continuing researches of Dr. Osis and others, actual sightings of apparitions seem to be on the decline. In contrast to the Society for Psychical Research in its heyday, today's research into psychic phenomena receives little attention from the world at large.

Dr. Ian Stevenson, head of the Division of Personality Studies at the University of Virginia Medical School, offers two possible avenues of explanation. First, Stevenson contends that it is necessary to determine if there are, in fact, as many apparitional experiences occurring in the world now as formerly. If there are as many cases, why are fewer of them reported? Social conditions, Stevenson suggests, provide at least part of the explanation. When we think of phantoms we almost automatically think of an earlier age; our modern world seems to prohibit such things. Perhaps this climate of disbelief renders people less likely to admit to having had apparitional encounters.

Suppose, on the other hand, that there actually are fewer encounters taking place in the present. If this is the case, Stevenson reasons, perhaps it is also a function of the differences in the eras. First, communications are far more sophisticated now than formerly. In many of the cases collected in the past by the researchers, the percipient had not seen the apparent in many months and often had a desperate need to do so. This urgency may have been a factor in producing apparitions. The more modern communications of today make such a situation less likely, however. Second, the incidence of sudden death is far lower now than it was in the Victorian era, a circumstance that might also contribute to the seeming paucity of phantom encounters. Finally, the same social conditions that might prohibit people from reporting apparitional experiences may inhibit phantoms from appearing.

Even so, some recent experiences, such as the crisis apparition reported by Hilde Saxer in a small village in the South Tyrol, could have happened only during the modern age. On May 4, 1980, Hilde left her job at a local restaurant at her usual time of 11:30 P.M. As the woman began her walk home, she happened to see the distinctive gray Audi belonging to her sister's fiancé, Johann Hofer. The sight surprised her somewhat, because Johann had left the restaurant half an hour earlier, stressing that he needed to go directly home. There was no question that the car was his, however, and when Hilde waved, she saw Johann through the windshield. The young man slowed his car, smiled, and waved back as he passed.

An hour later, Johann's father heard him arrive home at his normal time. The father clearly heard the sound of his son's engine, and he recognized the noise of the distinctive turning maneuver the young man used to get his car into the family yard.

Neither Hilde or Mr. Hofer realized that anything was amiss until the next day, when it was discovered that Johann was nowhere to be found. Although news came over the radio of a major tunnel collapse on the route Johann usually traveled to get home, no one thought anything of it; after all, he had been seen by Hilde and heard by his father shortly after the cave-in.

But as the day wore on and Johann failed to appear, his father began to fear the worst. It was many days before Johann's gray Audi, crushed flat beneath tons of falling rock, could be recovered, and even then his family and friends could scarcely believe the truth. Throughout the ordeal they had comforted themselves with one thought: The tunnel had collapsed at 11:30 P.M., and Johann had been spotted alive afterward.

Both Miss Saxer and Mr. Hofer seemed to have experienced crisis apparitions, made all the more interesting by the importance of Johann's car in helping to document the psychic encounter.

For all its modern trappings, this case seems thoroughly congruent with the body of evidence accumulated in the hundred-plus years since the SPR was formed. Like so many other reports, it is both elusive and tantalizing. Thus, investigators can only press on. Long ago, Frederic Myers offered a rueful summary of the situation: It is the lot of such researchers, he wrote, "to be working (however imperfectly) in the main track of discovery, and assailing a problem which, though strange and hard, does yet stand next in order among the new adventures on which Science must needs set forth."

# Phantoms in the Family

If sheer quantity of ghosts is any indication, the world's most haunted family may well be the Bowes Lyons, earls of Strathmore. Their ancestral home, in County Angus, Scotland, is the dour and daunting Glamis Castle, a menacing edifice that Shakespeare chose as the setting for *Macbeth.* Indeed, the eleventh-century Scottish king Malcolm II was stabbed to death in Glamis, and his blood is still said to stain the floor in one of the castle's innumerable rooms. Glamis's many ghosts include a lady in gray, a small black boy, and a Strathmore earl who supposedly lost a card game with the devil. Also supposed to dwell in the castle is the shade of a monstrously deformed child who was once locked away by the family in a hidden room.

Though particularly replete with tales of ghosts, the Strathmores are by no means unique. The British Isles teem with stories of specters associated with specific counties, houses, or families. These wandering spirits may be explained away as shared imaginings that have been promoted by fireside tales and handed down through the years. But the fact remains that reported sightings of family ghosts persist, often related by reliable witnesses, through decades and even generations. Some stories tell of phantoms who seem to be kindly disposed toward their host families or, at worst, indifferent. But far more often, the appearance of the familial shade is said to augur death for a family member. Most family ghosts are harbingers of doom.

## A Red-Haired Revenant

Ireland abounds with tales of the banshee, a wailing creature whose visitation marks death. Her name in Gaelic is *bansidhe*—fairy woman—although most say she is not a fairy but a spirit who is sometimes benevolent, sometimes malign. Banshees are linked by centuries-old legends to the great houses of Ireland, whose misfortunes are chronicled in the spirits' mournful cries or fiendish laughter.

In the seventeenth century, Lady Ann Fanshawe, visiting her friend Lady Honora O'Brien in Ireland, was awakened one night by an eerie voice. She peered through a window and saw a woman who seemed to hover just outside the glass. The phantom's body trailed into the mist, but her face, limned in moonlight, was clear—pale, green eyed, and lovely, framed by masses of red-gold hair. The apparition moaned three times, and then sighed and vanished.

When Lady Ann told her hostess of the flame-haired apparition the next morning, Lady Honora showed neither surprise nor alarm. She explained that centuries before, a young woman was seduced and murdered by the castle's owner and her body buried beneath the room where Lady Ann had slept. One might wonder why the girl chose to attach herself to a family that had so mistreated her; nevertheless, Lady Honora said, the young victim became a banshee who would appear when any O'Brien died. Floating outside the window above her grave, she would keen for the family member's passing. The banshee's appearance the previous night was no mystery to Lady Honora; at about the time Lady Ann saw the apparition, her hostess's cousin had died in the castle.

**A Malicious Monk** The ghost of a spiteful monk who delighted in misfortune was said to haunt Newstead Abbey, Nottinghamshire, England, the ancestral home of the colorful Byron family.

The abbey was the priory of the Black Augustine canons for almost 400 years. But in the sixteenth century King Henry VIII, angry with the Roman Catholic church for opposing the annulment of his marriage to Catherine of Aragon, began confiscating church lands and parceling out some of them to his nobles. Newstead Abbey fell to the Byrons and remained in the family for the next 300 years. The last Lord Byron to inherit it was none other than the Romantic poet and handsome rakehell, George Gordon, who not only loved the estate but found fodder for his verse in the the most notable of its several ghosts, the Black Friar.

No one knows who this restless soul might have been in life, but some believe that his shade, cowled and dark visaged, represented the church's curse on usurpers of its lands. Certainly the Black Friar seemed ill-disposed toward the Byrons. Legend tells that when a family member died, the phantom monk would make a visit to gloat at the tragedy. Conversely, it would present a sorrowful face at happy occasions such as births. The appearance of the grief-stricken mien was the norm at most family weddings as well—but not all. The poet Lord Byron averred he saw the ghost looking cheerful enough at his own marriage to Annabella Milbanke, which he would come to describe as the unhappiest event of his life.

In his *Don Juan,* Byron alludes to the Black Friar:

> By the marriage-bed of their lords, 'tis said,
> He flits on the bridal eve;
> And 'tis held as faith, to their bed of death
> He comes—but not to grieve.

## An Unnatural Daughter

Berry Pomeroy, a castle in South Devon, England, that dates back to the Tudor period, has fallen into ruin, but it is still said to house many ghosts. Among them is that of a beautiful young woman who was doomed by her own wickedness.

Her name was Margaret, daughter of an early baron of Pomeroy. She bore a child by her father and then strangled the infant. After her own death, her ghost was said to herald deaths among the Pomeroys and their retainers.

Among the many who supposedly saw her was Sir Walter Farquhar, an eminent physician of the late eighteenth century. While at Berry Pomeroy attending the ailing wife of the castle's steward, Sir Walter caught sight of a stunning young woman, who was wringing her hands in obvious distress. She started up a stairway and then paused and turned briefly toward the doctor. He saw her clearly in the light streaming through a stained-glass window before she vanished into one of the upper rooms.

The next day, Sir Walter asked the steward who the beautiful visitor on the staircase had been. To the doctor's immense surprise, the man cried out that he was sure her visit meant that his wife was dying. He related how Margaret had killed her child in the room above the staircase and how her ghost had ever since presaged the deaths of castle inmates, including that of his own son. The doctor assured the steward that the condition of his wife, who was far from dying, was in fact much better. Nevertheless, the steward would not be comforted. His wife died at noon that same day.

**A Tortured Cat** The manor house of Oxenby in England, erected during the reign of Edward VI, was a gloomy building, faced with flint and buttressed with gray stone. Its ill-lit interior was not unlike "a subterranean chapel or charnel house," according to a schoolmistress named Mrs. Hartnoll, who had lived there as a girl.

According to the late Elliott O'Donnell, a former pupil of Mrs. Hartnoll's and a collector of ghostlore, the lady was a no-nonsense sort, not a person given to fantasy. But even she ascribed a pervasive eeriness to the old house. She told O'Donnell that one day she was walking along one of its shadowy corridors when a door creaked open and a huge black cat crept slowly through it. The creature had been horribly maltreated. One of its eyes and a hind paw were missing. It seemed to want comfort, but as it fell at the girl's feet it somehow vanished into the floor. That evening, the future schoolmistress's brother was killed in an accident.

She did not see the spectral cat again for another two years. Then it appeared to her near the same cobwebbed spot where she had first seen it. As before, the pathetic animal was maimed and bleeding, apparently in its death throes. That same day, the girl's mother died of a stroke. Nearly four years later the cat appeared to the girl yet once more, and by evening the father of the family was dead.

The manor's dark history includes the chilling tale of an orphaned boy whose father had once owned the estate. The monstrous guardian who had been named to care for the lad finally murdered his ward and tried to install as heir his own illegitimate son—but not before forcing the true heir to watch while he and his bastard mutilated and boiled the boy's pet cat.

**A Horrific Hag** Undoubtedly the most repulsive of Great Britain's omen ghosts is the Gwrach-y-rhibyn, a phantom that belongs exclusively to Wales.

Her name literally means "hag of the mist," but it is more commonly translated "hag of the dribble" or "dribbling hag." She is said to appear as a hideous old woman who features masses of matted hair, a beak nose, penetrating eyes, and tusklike teeth. Her long arms end in clawed fingers, and scaly black wings that are as leathery as a bat's sprout from the middle of her crooked back. Different as she looks from Ireland's lovely banshee, the Hag of the Dribble keens and cries like the Irish spirit and has a similar function: She foretells death. The fearsome apparition is believed to serve as doom's emissary to families of old Welsh blood. Some Welsh inhabitants claim actually to have seen her gorgonlike visage. Others know the ominous crone as a dry rasp of claws on a windowpane or a baleful swish of wings that are too large for any bird.

One ancient family said to be haunted by the Gwrach-y-rhibyn was that of the Stradlings of South Wales. For 700 years, until the middle of the eighteenth century, the Stradlings occupied Saint Donat's Castle on the seashore of Glamorgan. The family eventually lost the estate, although, it seems, the Dribbling Hag continued to associate Saint Donat's with the Stradlings.

One night a guest at the castle awoke to the sound of a woman wailing and moaning beneath his window. He looked outside, but darkness veiled whatever lurked there. Then he heard a tapping against the window, followed by the flapping of enormous wings. Some eldritch quality in the sounds so frightened the visitor that he crept back to bed, but only after lighting a lamp to burn until morning. By the light of day, the guest asked his hostess if her sleep the previous night had been troubled by strange moans and scratchings. She replied that it had and that she knew the creature who made the noises was the Gwrach-y-rhibyn. As if to confirm her words, news soon came to the castle that the last direct descendant of the Stradling family was dead.

**A Disembodied Arm** According to legend, one branch of Scotland's MacKenzie clan is haunted by a spectral hand that manifests itself only under the grimmest of circumstances: Its appearance always signals the imminent death of a family member.

The ghost has been seen well into the twentieth century. On one occasion it supposedly materialized from the wall of a movie theater while a MacKenzie sat in the audience. In another instance, the arm reputedly appeared to a young woman in the family as she was about to leave her bedroom one morning. Hearing something bang to the floor behind her, she turned and saw that a tall silver candlestick—a solid and heavy piece—had somehow fallen off a chest of drawers. She bent to pick it up, wondering what could have dislodged it. Suddenly she saw, protruding from the wall, a hand and forearm. The milk-white arm disappeared into the wall at the elbow. Its slender hand had tapering fingers and almond-shaped nails and clearly belonged to a woman. Just as clearly, it had pushed the candlestick from its perch to the floor. Even as the young woman stared at it, the ghostly appendage slowly vanished. Knowing that the phantom hand played the role of death's messenger for the family, she feared for the life of her mother, who had been quite ill. Her qualms proved groundless, however; the mother recovered. But only a few days after the candlestick fell, the family received news that a cousin had died.

**An Ominous Bird** Sir James Oxenham of Devon was in a merry mood—so the story goes—and with good cause. It was the night before the marriage of his only child, his beautiful daughter Margaret, and scores of guests had come to feast in her honor. She was marrying the man of her choice, a promising youth who was much to Sir James's liking. Both families were pleased, in fact, and celebration was the order of the evening.

Sir James was making an expansive speech, thanking the guests for their attendance, when suddenly he paled and stuttered to a halt. Alarm rustled through the audience, but at last he recovered his self-possession. He went on with the speech, but its former joviality was missing, and he hastened toward a conclusion. After the banquet, Sir James confided to a trusted servant the reason for his distress. As he was speaking, the nobleman said, he saw a white-breasted bird appear, seemingly from nowhere, and fly toward Margaret. It circled her several times and then flew away. The servant needed no further explanation, since he knew well the story that a phantom bird had long haunted the Oxenham family. At least since the sixteenth century, and probably much earlier, the white bird had been seen to hover near the deathbeds of Oxenhams. For generations it had been the family's harbinger of death. The servant tried to comfort his master, but it was no use. Sir James said he knew that Margaret was in mortal peril.

The nobleman's fears proved to be well founded. No sooner had the marriage service begun the next morning than an altar tapestry billowed out and a man who had been hiding behind it thrust his dagger through the fabric of Margaret's wedding gown and into her heart. She fell dead at the feet of her horrified groom. The assassin, a rejected suitor of the bride's, then stabbed himself to death with the bloody knife.

**A Headless Horseman** In Scotland members of the MacLaine clan from the district of Lochbuie shun the nocturnal sound of clattering hooves and a jingling bridle. They fear the sight of a spectral horse bearing a headless rider who forebodes death.

The name of the rider is Ewen of the Little Head. Ewen was the son and heir of a MacLaine chief, but the son envied the father's wealth and fell to feuding with him. There was much inconclusive bickering between the two men, and at last both parties sought to settle the matter by force of arms. In 1538 father and son led their partisans into battle, and the son was beheaded by one of his father's followers. From that time into the twentieth century, many witnesses have told how the headless Ewen rides to harvest the souls of Lochbuie MacLaines.

Ironically, this messenger of doom supposedly had a deadly omen of his own. According to one story, on the evening before the fatal skirmish, Ewen met up with the Faery Washing-Woman, a Scottish folklore figure akin to the Irish banshee and the Welsh Hag of the Dribble. On the eve of battles, it was her dire function to wash blood from the garments of combatants who were destined to die. Ewen was walking along a stream when he saw the old woman crouched by the water, rinsing a pile of blood-stained shirts. He asked her if his own shirt was there, and the hag replied that it was. But he might avoid his doom, she added, if the next morning his wife, with no prompting, served him butter with breakfast. Unfortunately, Ewen's wife was an indifferent cook, and no butter appeared on the table. The luckless man stoically munched his dry bread, then rode to battle that morning knowing he would not ride home that night.

***Legend claims that King Charles I of England (below) might have avoided defeat at the 1645 battle of Naseby if he had heeded the advice of a ghostly visitor: the late Thomas Wentworth, Earl of Strafford (right).***

on the side of the agent. In the 313 cases, motivation was strong for the agents in 248 and moderate in 69, while remaining weak in only 40. Among the percipients, the reverse was true; motivation was strong or moderate in only 64 cases but weak in 298. (In some cases, there was more than one agent and more than one percipient.) Gibson found it interesting that the vast majority of alleged communications were between family members and friends; only a little more than 15 percent occurred between strangers and casual acquaintances.

As an example of a case in which the motivation rested almost entirely with the phantom, Gibson cited a collective encounter that involved a girl, one of two daughters, who was suddenly awakened in the night by feelings of dread and horror. She saw nothing in the room, but her terror was so overwhelming that she spent the rest of the night huddled under the blankets.

The next morning, she met her mother, who looked strangely pale and drawn, coming downstairs. The mother at first refused to discuss the matter. Eventually, though, she related that she too had been awakened in the night. She heard her bedroom door opening, she said, and saw, to her horror, her other daughter, Susan, enter in her nightdress. "She came straight toward my bed, turned down the clothes, and laid herself beside me, and I felt a cold chill all down my side where she seemed to touch me. I suppose I fainted, . . . and when I came to myself the apparition had gone—but of one thing I am sure, and that is *that it was not a dream.*" The family subsequently heard that Susan had died that night in a hospital some distance away and that just before her death she had talked of returning home.

Gibson cited a number of instances in which the phantom had appeared anywhere from several days to many weeks after the person's death. In one case, the apparition reportedly was observed by no fewer than eight people who were, wrote Gibson, "either affected by mass hallucination or had entered the field of a strong psychical occurrence, and were affected by it despite wide variations in intensity of rapport with the supposed agent."

The incident took place in London in May 1873 and involved a Captain Towns, who had died six weeks before in Sydney, Australia. On this day, the captain's middle-aged daughter happened to go into one of the bedrooms of her home, accompanied by a young woman visitor. There, according to the daughter's husband, who related the tale, "they were amazed to see, reflected as it were on the polished surface of the wardrobe, the image of Captain Towns. It was barely half figure, the head, shoulders, and part of the arms only showing—in fact, it was like an ordinary medallion portrait, but life-size. The face appeared wan and pale, . . . and he wore a kind of grey flannel jacket, in which he had been accustomed to sleep. Surprised and half alarmed at what they saw, their first idea was that a portrait had been hung in the room and what they saw was its reflection—but there was no picture of the kind."

At that point, the daughter's sister entered the room, and before the other two had a chance to speak, she exclaimed, "Good gracious! Do you see papa?" One of the housemaids happened by at that moment and was asked if she saw anything. "Oh, miss! The master," she gasped. The captain's old body servant was summoned, and he immediately cried, "Oh, Lord save us! Mrs. Lett, it's the captain!" The butler was called next, then a nursemaid, and both saw it. Finally, the old captain's grieving widow was sent for. "Seeing the apparition," related the daughter's husband, "she advanced toward it with arms extended as if to touch

it, and as she passed her hand over the panel of the wardrobe the figure gradually faded away, and never again appeared." Added the husband: "It was by the merest accident that I did not see the apparition. I was in the house at the time, but did not hear when I was called."

Unlike many post-mortem cases, the captain appeared to leave no message, and he gave no indication of his motive for appearing before so many people half a world away from his resting place. Perhaps, some have mused, he merely wished all of his family and servants to see him, and he them, one more time.

In another case, famous for the evidence offered, the apparition seemed to have a compelling reason for appearing. The percipient was a businessman, identified as F.G., whose sister had died of cholera nine years before, at the age of eighteen. On this day, F.G. was on a business trip, resting in his hotel room in St. Joseph, Missouri, when he suddenly became aware of a figure beside him in the room. F.G. was amazed to see his long-deceased sister and was particularly surprised to note that her face was disfigured by a long red scratch on the cheek. After displaying herself and her injury, the apparition vanished.

Returning home, F.G. reported the incident to his mother, who nearly collapsed. Upon regaining her composure, the woman confessed that when paying her last respects to her dead daughter, she had tried, as she put it, to "touch up" the face, and had somehow inflicted a scratch on the girl's cheek. To conceal the accident, she had then carefully covered the scratch with makeup. No one had known of it until the daughter's ghost appeared before the brother.

As with crisis apparitions, many brushes with post-mortem phantoms seem to stem from promises made in life. The case of David's promise to recover his friend Eddie's body from the mountain is a poignant one. There are others in which the promise has been mutual, as with "death compacts," agreements between two living people that the first to die will attempt to contact the survivor.

One of these cases, which reportedly took place in England in 1940, involved a young man who awoke early on a Sunday morning to find the figure of an unknown man standing at the foot of his bed. "He looked steadily at me with a smile," the young man later recalled. "Seeing the kindness in his eyes, I stopped being afraid and was completely master of myself again. Suddenly the man came straight up to me. If he had been a creature of flesh and blood he would, moving in that direction, have had to climb over the bed. But the man approached me as if the bed were not there, and without a word to me, passed by on my right, then through the wall and disappeared."

The young man had scarcely a moment to catch his breath before a second, even more startling vision appeared. This time he recognized the apparition. It was his best friend, who had died six weeks earlier. The two had made a death compact years before, each vowing that whoever died first was to return to shake hands with the other as a sign of life after death.

The apparition made no move to shake hands, however. Instead he simply stood at the foot of the bed and gazed solemnly at his friend for a long time before vanishing through the bedroom wall, as the earlier figure had done. "I know now," the young man later wrote, "that there is no death for us human beings."

Actually, in this reported occurrence it is difficult to determine whether the apparent or the percipient had the stronger motivation. The encounter could have been wish fulfillment on the part of the surviving friend, a fanciful image conjured up in his own mind to reassure himself of life in the hereafter. Certainly that motive would have been a strong one, but so too was that of the supposed apparent, who made a bargain in life that could be kept only in death.

What is intriguing about the case, aside from the partial consummation of the compact, is the identity of the older stranger. Some have suggested that he may have been a fellow phantom, sent by the deceased to test the waters, as it were, to see if the living friend was receptive before hazarding an appearance.

Motive is more readily suggested in the case involving

# Banishing Baneful Ghosts

To the Dogon people of West Africa, death is a kind of half-life, a shadowy, tenuous, unsettled existence. Nostalgic spirits of the dead are reportedly loath to leave their villages and slow to depart, even when their bodies lie close among ancestors' bones in burial grounds. Their impulse is to return home, meddlesome and querulous, disrupting households and bringing disease and drought.

So it is that Dogon burial ritual aims at hastening the spirit's adjustment to its diminished status. Funeral custom calls for young men of the tribe to dance. Each wears a mask, like the one shown at right, representing some part of life the deceased might miss—a tree, an animal, a person. Seeing these, the ghost can bid farewell and accept its new role as ancestral spirit. And, in so doing, it will be content to leave life to the living.

In the matter of keeping ghosts at bay, the Dogon are in no way unique. All over the world, from the Arctic Circle to the South Seas, fear of ghosts has worked its way into tribal and religious burial rituals, some of which are illustrated on the following pages. Mourners have variously appeased corpses or attacked them, coddled or mutilated them. But the goal has always been the same: to segregate the dead from the living. The most benign of such funeral customs involve placating the ghost so it does not become a malevolent haunt. In some rites, it is sufficient to request that the spirit stay away, or to plead with it, reason with it, or utter incantations against it. In other cultures, more is required. A common belief persisting in the West Indies is that a male ghost wants to return to be with his wife. Thus widows spend their period of mourning wearing red underwear, since red is thought to repel ghosts.

Another time-honored stratagem involves confusing a corpse so that once it is buried, its spirit will not be able to find its way home. However diverse geographically, certain tribes in South Africa, Asia, India, and Melanesia have shared a reluctance to use doors in carrying the dead to burial. Some Fiji islanders, for instance, still break down the side of a house for the corpse's egress, while Eskimos remove their dead through a dwelling's smoke hole or window. The purpose is to hide the real entrance from the deceased's spirit, discouraging its return.

Similar ploys, common to many cultures, have involved confusing a pursuing ghost by camouflaging or redirecting the route of a funeral cortege's homeward march. Prior to Communist collectivization in Siberia, Koryak tribespeople disguised not only their route but themselves as well. Followers in funeral processions tried to throw the ghost off the scent with animal sounds, cawing like crows and barking like foxes.

Some tribes have considered psychological deterrence insufficient and sought a more physical defense. Widowers in New Guinea still go through their mourning periods armed with an ax to ward off dead wives' spirits. Binding together the thumbs or big toes of bodies to hobble their spirits was long common in parts of Australia and India and is still done by Eskimos near the Bering Sea. Extending the principle, the Siberian Chukchi used to cut a corpse's throat to prevent its spirit's return.

But the mutilation approach surely reached its apogee with the aboriginal Kwearriburra of Queensland, Australia. Before the progressive Westernization of the aborigines—well into the twentieth century—the Kwearriburra cut off the corpse's head and roasted it in a fire on top of the grave. Once charred, the head was smashed into small bits, which were left in the hot coals. The Kwearriburra reasoned that the deceased's rising ghost, searching for its head, would be scorched into retreating to its grave.

Ghost-fear rituals have persisted longest among primitive, polytheistic peoples. Yet even in the industrial West, some such customs endure, although time has obscured their origins. Many Westerners still wear black for mourning, but few know the practice originally stemmed from the notion that black made the living invisible to the dead.

*A Nepali lama officiating in a dead man's home writes the name of the corpse on bamboo paper, then burns the paper (above). Other objects may be burned as well, both as offerings to the gods and as tokens of the soul's release to seek its next incarnation. This rite, one of several manifestations of ghost fear in Buddhist cultures of the Himalayas, is meant to assure that the spirit of the deceased will not linger to haunt the living. At right, the dead man's widow prepares her husband for cremation by putting yak butter in his eyes. As she annoints the body, she shouts at the spirit, adjuring it not to return as a ghost.*

*Straining at their burden, young Balinese men carry the remains of several corpses to the cremation ground in an elaborate tower. Along the way, the tower bearers twirl and jostle the structure to disorient the spirits inside and frustrate any attempt they might make to return home. Funeral rites are joyful events for the Balinese, who believe cremation frees the soul for reincarnation. Great sums are spent for the towers and the ornate sarcophagi in which the bodies are burned. For all the respect shown for the dead, however, spirits must be discouraged from clinging to their previous lives and making a nuisance of themselves among survivors.*

*A dancing Dogon tribesman, costumed as a warrior from the neighboring Fulani tribe, brandishes his spear at make-believe cattle rustlers during a funeral ceremony (far left). The Dogon live on broad West African savannahs, but their grasslands are bordered by precipitous sandstone cliffs. Hundreds of caves in the cliffs serve as Dogon burial grounds, which are littered with generations of bones (below, left). Using ropes thrown over beams embedded in the cliffs, tribespeople hoist their dead up some 200 feet for burial; disease victims are buried in special isolation caves, and there are separate caves for burying men, women, children, and stillborn babies.*

the Reverend Arthur Bellamy. In 1874, Bellamy's wife learned of the death of a childhood friend with whom she had made a death compact many years before. Though she had not heard from her friend for quite some time, Mrs. Bellamy became nervous at the thought that the agreement the two of them had made might now be fulfilled. She shared her fears with her husband, who had neither met the friend nor seen a photograph of her.

Two nights later, the Reverend Bellamy awoke from a sound sleep to see the figure of a woman sitting by the side of the bed where his wife slept. "Had I the pencil and the brush of a Millais," he reported later, "I could transfer to canvas an exact likeness of the ghostly visitant. I remember that I was much struck, as I looked intently at her, with the careful arrangement of her coiffure, every single hair being most carefully brushed down."

After a time, the figure vanished. Bellamy lay in bed until his wife awoke and then described the ghostly visitor to her in great detail. The description perfectly matched Mrs. Bellamy's recollection of the friend with whom she had made the compact, but her husband wanted to be certain. "Was there any special point to strike one in her appearance?" he inquired. "Yes," his wife replied, "we girls used to tease her at school for devoting so much time to the arrangement of her hair." That detail, which Bellamy could not have known through any ordinary channel, convinced both him and his wife that the compact had been fulfilled.

The case is remarkable also because the apparition, which appeared some time after the agent's death, showed itself to someone other than the person principally concerned with the death compact. Clearly, Bellamy had only a passing interest in the compact's realization, and his own imagination could not have supplied the subtle detail of the apparition's carefully arranged hairstyle. In this instance, then, it would appear that the strongest motivation behind the occurrence belonged to the apparition itself.

Comparatively few post-mortem apparitional experiences involve death compacts. More often the evident reasons for a phantasm's appearance are highly emotional, involving love, concern, or—as in one notable case—disappointment over a neglected promise.

This case involved a man who had suffered complications from a hernia operation in 1911 and died of pneumonia soon afterward. Before his death, his daughter, Josephine, promised to burn a so-called soul light—actually an oil and wax candle—in his memory for one year.

One day, as Josephine sat having lunch with her own children, a persistent rapping noise drifted into the room from upstairs. The noise seemed to originate in the room that had been her father's and where his soul light now burned. The children became frightened as the eerie knocking continued. Before long, Josephine went off to find the source. "We all listened intently," one of the children, John, reported, "and we heard our mother's voice as well as our grandfather's—we could not possibly have been mistaken, even though we were unable to understand what they were saying." After a minute or two, Josephine returned to the lunch table in a state of obvious agitation, her eyes reddened with tears. The family members finished their meal in silence. Try as they might, the children could not get their mother to say anything about what or whom she had found in the room. Afterward, however, Josephine drew John, her son, aside and asked him to run to the village at once to buy a quart of oil for her father's light.

Only much later did John learn the truth of what had happened that day: "I went into grandfather's room," his mother eventually told him, "and there I saw him, dressed as he was when we put him into his coffin, standing upright near the cupboard. He had hardly caught sight of me when he said, . . . 'Josephine, why did you let the little light go out?' I replied that by mistake I had run out of oil, and he answered: 'My daughter, on no account must anyone ever break a promise once given. See that my light is burning again this very day.' "

Psychical literature abounds with tales of apparitions returning to remind the living of promises made in life. These promises, like that of Josephine's to her father, seem especially binding when made over a deathbed. Such agreements—as one C. Happerfield reportedly learned in a somewhat abrupt manner from the supposed spirit of his friend John Harford—know no time limit.

As he lay dying in June of 1851, Harford called Happerfield to his bedside and extracted a solemn promise that Happerfield would look after his widow. His mind greatly eased, Harford died a short time later.

True to his word, Happerfield set up Mrs. Harford in a small cottage and saw to her needs. Some time later, one of the widow's grandsons approached Happerfield and proposed to take her into his own home. Since Mrs. Harford seemed pleased by the idea, Happerfield agreed, content that he had done his duty according to his dying friend's wish.

One night, as Happerfield lay awake in bed thinking about some business matters, he became conscious of another presence in the room. Looking up, he saw the figure of his friend Harford standing before him, his face sorrowful and troubled. In a familiar but agitated voice, the apparition spoke out. "Friend Happerfield," it said, "I have come to you because you have not kept your promise to see to my wife. She is in trouble and in want."

*Invisible to all but the accused, the ghost of a murdered man confronts his slayer in this eighteenth-century engraving of a trial in London. Tales of spectral justice are common in psychic annals.*

Startled, Happerfield assured the phantasm that he had not been aware of any difficulty but would inquire immediately. This seemed to satisfy the apparition, who stepped backward into the shadows and vanished.

In the morning, Happerfield wrote to the grandson who had taken in Harford's widow. The young man quickly replied, saying that he had lost his schoolmaster position and could no longer support his elderly grandmother. In fact, he had been on the point of committing her to a public institution. Happerfield felt the sting of conscience over the promise that he had broken, however unwittingly. At once, he sent money so that Mrs. Harford could return to his care. If not for the intervention of Harford's phantom, it seems, she might have died a pauper's death.

The motivating forces behind both the case of Harford's widow and that of the extinguished soul light are easily understood. Both alleged apparents clearly wished to remind the living of vows that they had neglected. The motivations of the percipients—Josephine and Happerfield—are less clear and probably less strong, since neither knew beforehand of the lapsed promise.

The experience of Lucy Dodson offers a fresh perspective on such questions. As in the previous stories, Lucy had no prior knowledge of the circumstances that inspired the encounter. But in this case the apparition seemingly appeared not to fulfill a promise but to seek one.

On a Sunday evening, June 5, 1887, Lucy was in her bedroom when she heard her name being called. Incredibly, the voice seemed to be that of her mother, who had been dead for sixteen years. Somewhat fearfully, Lucy called out her mother's name. As Lucy related the incident, an apparition of Mrs. Dodson then appeared, bearing two small babies in her arms.

Placing the children in her daughter's arms, the figure spoke to her. "Lucy," it said, "promise me to take care of them, for their mother is just dead." The phantom paused and seemed to fix Lucy with a beseeching gaze. "Promise me to take care of them," it implored. Lucy quickly agreed to the earnest request and urged her mother to stay and speak further. "Not yet, my child," said the apparition. And then it vanished.

Lucy sat holding the children in her arms for a time before falling asleep. When she awoke, the children were gone. And she soon received a grim message—her sister-in-law had died after giving birth to a second child. Lucy, who had not known of the younger child's birth, immediately volunteered to care for the children.

In other instances, phantoms seem to return in hopes of atoning for some wrong done in life. One young woman reported such an experience to the Society for Psychical Research that seems all the more remarkable for having occurred in the middle of a bright summer day. It happened as she was working in her kitchen, the woman claimed. She

# Portrait of a Lady

Although writer Charles Dickens had little patience with the Victorian passion for spiritualism, he loved to write about the supernatural. One such narrative, published with three others under the title "Four Ghost Stories" in the periodical *All the Year Round,* developed into a real-life ghost story so eerie that it evidently convinced even its skeptical author that he had had a brush with the paranormal.

Dickens's 1861 tale concerns a society portrait painter, Mr. H., who, while traveling to a country estate on September 13, meets a delicate-looking young lady on the train. After some conversation, she asks him if he can paint a person from memory. The artist replies that he is not certain but it may be possible.

"Well," says the woman, "look at me again. You may have to take a likeness of me." Mr. H. studies her face carefully, and then the travelers go their separate ways.

Two years later, a Mr. Wylde comes to call on the painter and asks if it is possible for him to paint a portrait based only on a description. The visitor goes on to describe his daughter, two years dead, and requests a picture of her. The artist tries several unsuccessful sketches. Then, in a moment of inspiration, he draws the young woman he met on the train. "Instantly," wrote Dickens, "a bright look of recognition and pleasure lighted up the father's face, and he exclaimed, 'That is she!' "

The artist asks when it was that Mr. Wylde's daughter died, and the man replies: " 'Two years ago; on the 13th of September.' "

Within a few days of the story's publication, Dickens received a remarkable letter from a portrait painter who informed him that the tale printed in *All the Year Round* matched in astonishing detail a real experience of his own, one that he had written up for publication. The meeting with the young lady on the train and the later request from the bereaved father were all laid out in the real painter's account. The portraitist, naturally enough, believed that Dickens had somehow heard his story and beaten him to publication.

"In particular," wrote the aggrieved artist in his letter to Dickens, "how else was it possible that the date, the 13th of September, could have been got at? For I never told the date until I wrote it."

"Now *my* story," recounted Dickens in apparent wonder, "had NO DATE; but seeing, when I looked over the proofs, the great importance of having *a* date, I wrote in, unconsciously, the exact date on the margin of the proof!"

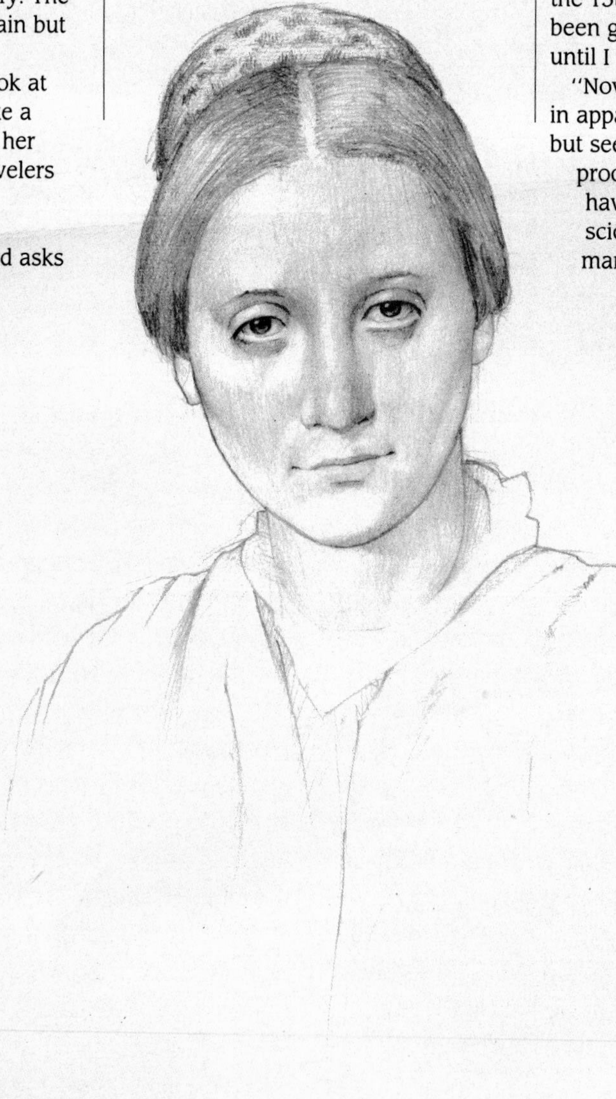

felt herself inexplicably drawn to the attic of her house. There she opened an old suitcase and withdrew a box of letters from her former fiancé, who had abruptly broken their engagement six years earlier. Though distraught at the time, the young woman had seldom thought of her former love in recent years.

In the midst of reading through the letters, she found herself suddenly overwhelmed with pity for the young man, although she could not understand the reason. At that moment she looked up and beheld him standing in front of her. For some time the young man stood silently. Then quietly, but with a sense of suppressed urgency, he said, "You must forgive me everything I did to you; I was a poor creature." Feeling mesmerized by his presence and his words, the young woman granted her forgiveness. At this, she said, the figure dissolved into the air.

It was not until the next day that the young woman learned, through a notice in the newspaper, of her former fiancé's death. He had died on the same afternoon that his phantasm had appeared to her.

In this case, too, the apparition seems to have been motivated by a promise that had been made—or rather, broken—in life. Apparently troubled by the unhappiness he had caused, the young man returned in ghostly form in order to seek forgiveness from the one person who could ease his troubled conscience.

A similar case was reported in Russia in the late nineteenth century. It concerned one Basil von Driesen, who had not been on very good terms with his father-in-law, Nicholas Ponomareff. At the time of the older man's final illness, relations between the two were civil but cool. Nine days after Ponomareff's death, as von Driesen sat reading by candlelight, he heard the sound of footsteps in the adjacent room. The sound ceased just outside the closed door of his bedroom. Von Driesen called out but received no answer. However, he soon saw, he claimed later, the form of his father-in-law standing inside the closed bedroom door. "It was he undoubtedly," von Driesen wrote, "in his blue dressing gown, lined with squirrel furs and only half buttoned, so that I could see his white waistcoat and his black trousers . . . . I was not frightened. They say that, as a rule, one is *not* frightened when seeing a ghost, as ghosts possess the quality of paralyzing fear."

The figure of Ponomareff did not reply immediately when his son-in-law spoke to him. Instead, he stepped forward and paused near the bed, his face fixed with an expression of uneasiness and concern. "I have acted wrongly toward you," the apparition said at last. "Forgive me! Without this I do not feel at rest there." The figure extended his right hand. Von Driesen shook the hand, which he described as "long and cold," and gave his forgiveness. At once the figure withdrew. "I fell asleep," von Driesen claimed, "with the sense of joy which a man who has done his duty must feel."

The need for forgiveness is a common thread that runs through many tales of apparitional experiences, but such occurrences are surely open to a certain amount of skepticism. In the case of von Driesen, for instance, did his imagination merely conjure the show of forgiveness he himself may have desired? A researcher might conclude that both the apparent and the percipient had equal motivation for the encounter.

More striking are the cases in which the percipient has little or no motivation for seeing a phantom, such as the one involving Thomas Erskine, one of Great Britain's most brilliant lawyers and later a Lord Chancellor and member of Parliament. Erskine, who died in 1823, once related an incident from his youth that even his supremely logical mind could not explain.

Erskine had been away from his native Scotland for some time. On returning to Edinburgh, he happened to see his former family butler in the street. The butler, Erskine reported, looked pale and shadowy. Erskine called out to the man and inquired after his current business. "To meet your honor," the old man surprisingly replied, "and to solicit your interference with my lord to recover a sum due to me, which the steward at the last settlement did not pay."

Struck by the butler's obvious distress, Erskine beck-

# Revenge of the Spectral Tiger

Solitary and powerful, combining blurring speed with lethal grace, the tiger is a creature of awesome proportions. Understandably, it has figured prominently in the beliefs of those living most closely with it, inhabitants of India, China, and Southeast Asia. Often the tiger was said to be possessed, or to form a strange alliance with ghosts or demons. Near Assam, India, for example, a phantom tiger, Bengala, allegedly guarded graves and shrines.

Illustrating the tiger's appeal is the story supposedly told to British author and ghost hunter Elliott O'Donnell by an acquaintance who had lived in India. This man, called Colonel De Silva in O'Donnell's narrative, described how he saw an enormous tiger kill an old leper. De Silva could only stand by helplessly while the dying man cursed him and his family for not coming to his aid.

About a year afterward, continued the narrator, "rumors of a man-eater having been at work again were spread about us." Inexplicably, those who were only wounded then developed leprosy, leading locals to claim that the tiger was in league with the spirit of the dead leper. De Silva managed to shoot the tiger once, but encountered the ghostly white creature again as it stalked his wife, child, and the child's nurse. "I must fire at all costs," recounted De Silva. "If mortal, I must kill it, if ghostly, the noise of my rifle might dematerialize it." He shot just as the tiger sprang at the three terrified people. The animal vanished, but not before the nurse died of shock and the little boy received a claw scratch on his cheek. Soon afterward, the child developed leprosy and died.

The phantom tiger, according to De Silva, was seen no more.

oned him into a bookseller's shop, where they might discuss the matter more privately than in the street. Erskine led the way, but when he turned back, the butler was gone.

Perplexed by the disappearance, Erskine went at once to the butler's quarters, where he found the man's wife in mourning. Her husband had died months before, she told the lawyer. On his deathbed he had spoken of money he was owed and assured her that his former master would seek justice on her behalf. Greatly impressed by the experience, Erskine saw the matter put right immediately. Having been out of the city for a long time, he had had no idea that he apparently had been speaking to a dead man when he engaged the butler in conversation, nor had he heard of the old man's troubles through any other channels.

Researchers believe that such reported encounters, in which previously unknown information is communicated to the percipient, afford valuable insight into the nature and motivation of apparitions. Often these cases, many of which involve phantoms seeking justice, provide the most dramatic illustrations of purposeful psychic phenomena on record—some involving blackmail, revenge, or, as in the case related by Romer Troxell, murder.

In 1970, Troxell drove from his home in Pennsylvania to Portage, Indiana, on a grim errand: to identify and claim the body of his son Charlie, who had been found murdered by the side of a deserted road.

From the moment he entered the town, Troxell reported later, he thought he heard a voice inside his head—the voice of his dead son seeming to give him directions. The next day, at the urging of the voice, Troxell went for a drive in the nearby city of Gary, looking for his son's missing car. Charlie's voice told him exactly where to go, and Troxell followed the instructions to the letter.

Any doubts that Troxell may have had about his sanity vanished when he saw his son's yellow car flash past him, going in the opposite direction. Making a U-turn, Troxell followed the car down a crowded street. In his fury, the bereaved father wanted to ram his son's car with his own vehicle but contented himself with following the other car until the driver stopped and got out. Pulling alongside the stolen car, Troxell hopped out and confronted the driver. Soon the police arrived and arrested the driver of the car, who was later charged with Charlie's murder.

"Charlie left me after we caught the killer," Troxell maintained. "He's in peace now." Police obviously could not confirm Troxell's claim of ghostly guidance. But a detective assigned to the case maintained that "Troxell did a fine job in solving our murder. We're grateful to him."

Such dramatic quests for justice are relatively rare among accounts of phantom activity. Often the only discernible reason for a ghost's appearance is utterly mundane; one helpful apparition is said to have manifested himself to his surviving son in order to help in the repairs of a troublesome towboat engine. Mundane or not, encounters among close family members appear to be the most common of all apparitional experiences, frequently involving even those people who resist the very idea of such phenomena, as in the case of the Reverend Russell H. Conwell.

As a noted lecturer and the founder of Temple University in Philadelphia, Conwell was one of the most prominent American clergymen of the late nineteenth century. By his own admission, however, he was not terribly receptive to what he called "spiritualistic rubbish." Yet, late in his life, Conwell reported a series of encounters of his own that he could not discredit.

In the early 1900s, shortly after his wife's death, Conwell experienced a recurring vision in which his late wife appeared every morning and sat smiling at the foot of his bed. The vision appeared so regularly and seemed so lifelike, even engaging in conversation with him, that Conwell resolved to put it to a test.

"I know you aren't really there," Conwell said one day as the apparition made its customary appearance. "Oh, but I am!" his wife's cheerful voice reportedly replied. "How can I be sure?" Conwell asked. "Are you willing that I should test you?" The smiling figure nodded. "All right," said Conwell, "tomorrow I will ask you a question."

*Romer Troxell displays a photo of his murdered son Charlie. The day after he saw his son's body in the morgue, said Troxell, Charlie's voice directed him to his killer. Local police confirmed that Troxell had solved the case.*

The next morning, Conwell, who was a Civil War veteran, asked the apparition for the location of his discharge paper from the Union Army. He had not seen it for years and felt certain that the apparition could not know where it was.

Yet the figure of his wife responded instantly. "It is in the black japanned box behind the books in your library."

Conwell rose from bed and went straight to the library. After some searching, he found the black laquered box hidden away at the back of a dusty bookshelf. Inside was the discharge paper.

Still, Conwell remained unconvinced. Perhaps, he reasoned, the location of the paper had been at the back of his mind all along, and he had only imagined that his wife's spirit had told him. He decided to devise another test. That day he instructed the housemaid, Mary, to hide his gold fountain pen, which had been a gift from his wife, and to be careful not to let him know where it was. The maid dutifully carried out the peculiar instruction.

When the figure of Mrs. Conwell next appeared, her husband posed his question. "Do you know where Mary hid my pen?" he asked. The apparition seemed to smile almost playfully. "Of course," it said. "Come with me." Conwell rose from his bed and followed his wife's phantom to a hall closet. "There," said the apparition confidently, gesturing toward the top shelf.

Conwell climbed a chair and ran his hand across the shelf but felt nothing. Convinced that the whole affair had been a dream or a delusion, he turned to step down from the chair. Somewhat to his surprise, the apparition still stood behind him, gesturing emphatically at the closet shelf as though to say, "It is there! Look again!"

Once more Conwell ran his hand across the shelf. This time, to his amazement, he felt the pen. "I do not presume to draw conclusions," Conwell wrote afterward; "I feel no reticence in repeating the story, only a certain reluctance lest some readers should force into it an interpretation which I myself do not pretend to give . . . . And yet I speak only what I myself have seen."

Russell Conwell's account, though precise and carefully measured, gives no details as to the physical appearance of the phantom. But the case of Clive Stirland, an English metallurgist who claimed that in 1974 he encountered the phantom of his father, offers a vivid description.

As Stirland told his story, he was sitting alone in his house near Middlesbrough one evening when he felt "a most peculiar sudden jerk or jolt, almost physical in nature, as though my whole body moved convulsively relative to the surroundings, or vice versa."

Looking around, Stirland saw a vision of his father, who had died more than twenty years earlier, standing only six feet away. "In appearance," Stirland related, "he was filmy or misty, insubstantial, yet of natural color and stature, observable in clear detail; a blurred but distinct image as of an object viewed through the blades of a rotating electric fan. He was dressed in a grey short-sleeved shirt open at the neck as would have been natural to him when dressed casually around the house. This apparition, if that is the word, was surrounded by an aura of gold, silver, and bright blue rings, approximately three feet in diameter, . . . radiating a white silvery light into the surround."

The figure neither spoke nor gave any reason for its appearance, but Stirland reported being nearly overwhelmed by the palpable force of his father's personality. "It is difficult to describe my mental state at this point," Stirland admitted. "It was ruled by emotion, amazement, perplexity, joy, and love in a confused mixture."

The theme of dead parents returning to reassure or help their surviving children is a fairly frequent one in the annals of psychical experience. Perhaps the most unusual case involves a dentist in Butte, Montana. According to his account, the timely appearance of his mother's phantom actually saved him from colluding in a patient's suicide.

During a routine extraction, the dentist had been on the point of injecting his patient with novocaine when he had "the strangest experience in my life." Withdrawing the needle without administering the anesthetic, the dentist backed away from his examination chair and stepped into his laboratory. There, he later reported, the phantom of his mother appeared to him bearing an urgent warning. Novocaine, the apparition revealed, would kill his patient. "He wants to die in your chair," the figure continued, "so you will be blamed and his family will not lose his life insurance." Returning to his patient, the dentist asked him why he had not mentioned any problems with novocaine. The patient then admitted that he had blacked out after a previous injection and that it had taken three doctors several hours to bring him back to consciousness.

Encounters with the apparition of one's mother are commonplace, though few are of such striking consequence. But a similar experience opened an entirely new avenue of psychical research and led Julian Burton to find his life's work.

In 1980 Burton was in California pursuing his Ph.D. in psychology when his studies took a dramatic turn. One evening in September, while entertaining relatives, Burton had gone into the kitchen to slice a pineapple. He heard what he thought were his wife's footsteps behind him. Turning to ask her a question, he confronted the phantom of his mother, who had died seven years earlier.

"She was fully visible," he wrote later, "looking years younger than at the time of her death. She was wearing a diaphanous pale-blue gown trimmed in marabou, which I had never seen before."

Before Burton could even call out, the figure of his mother disappeared, leaving him deeply unsettled. The next morning he called his sister, who added a further strange detail: Two weeks before her death, Mrs. Burton had gone shopping with her daughter and admired a pale-blue gown whose description perfectly matched that of the gown worn by the apparition. Burton was now convinced that he had had a genuine apparitional experience. As a result, he decided to devote his doctoral studies to psychical phenomena. "I felt that many people probably have similar experiences to tell," he recalled.

Accordingly, Burton devised a questionnaire, reminiscent of the *Census of Hallucinations* nearly a century earlier, asking respondents if they had ever had any psychical experiences. He began by distributing his questionnaire to members of psychic research and study groups in metropolitan Los Angeles. When his tally showed that 50 percent of the respondents claimed to have had contacts with the dead, he suspected that he was polling people who were predisposed to such experiences. But his rate of positive responses remained at the same level even after he broadened the pool of respondents to include psychology students at three Los Angeles colleges. Later studies continued to show high levels of these experiences, particularly among the elderly. In addition, Burton found that for many, the experiences had made such an impression that the percipients had changed their attitudes about death. Instead of a frightful end, they thought, it might actually be a bright beginning.

Dr. W. Dewi Rees, of Great Britain, is another of the psychologists who have explored death and survival. In 1971, Rees reported in the *British Medical Journal* on what he called "the hallucinations of widowhood." In polling 293 widows and widowers about their experiences after their spouses had died, Rees found that nearly half believed they had been in contact with their loved ones. However, Rees and his colleagues did not think their respondents were really communicating with the dead; they assumed the reported experiences were probably wish-fulfillment fantasies. Rees believed he had uncovered a new dimension to the mourning process, one suggesting that such experiences may be far more common than is generally known.

Even so, the question of whether reported post-mortem apparitional contacts are really evidence of human survival of death remains unanswered and may never be answered to the satisfaction of all researchers. But as long as the question is open, many well-known cases, such as the one reported by Mrs. Rosa Sutton, will continue to intrigue.

On October 11, 1907, the Portland, Oregon, woman received a letter from her son, James ("Jimmie"), a lieutenant on duty at the U.S. Naval Academy in Annapolis, Maryland. The letter was a cheerful one, but as she read it, Mrs. Sutton felt herself becoming nearly overwhelmed with feelings of distress and worry for her son. Later in the day, when she suffered an unexplainable attack of searing physical pain, Mrs. Sutton became convinced that her son was in danger. That evening, she shared her fears with members of her family, who did their best to reassure her.

The next day, however, the family received a telegram confirming Mrs. Sutton's worst fears. Jimmie was dead. According to details that arrived later, Lieutenant Sutton had been returning to the academy with some friends after a rowdy party when a fight broke out. Sutton was thrown to the ground. In a drunken rage, he threatened to kill his fellow officers and returned to his quarters to get his pistols. This led to his arrest, in the course of which he scuffled with his captors and evidently shot himself. An inquest later ruled the death a suicide.

Even before the news of the death had fully registered, Mrs. Sutton became aware of the figure of her son, draped in a long overcoat, hovering nearby. "At that instant," wrote Mrs. Sutton, "Jimmie stood right before me and said, 'Mamma, I never killed myself . . . . My hands are as free from blood as when I was five years old.' "

None of the other Sutton family members in the room at the time saw the apparition, causing Mr. Sutton to grow concerned that shock had thrown his wife into a hallucinatory state. Yet even as the family tried to calm her, Mrs. Sutton maintained that she continued to receive her son's message. He spoke, she said, of being attacked and beaten by a group of men. "A man hit me on the head with a butt of a gun so that I fell on my knees; then three of them jumped on me and beat me worse than a dog in the street and tried to run my face in the ground. They broke my watch with a kick . . . . They jumped on me with their feet, and I wonder that my ribs were not broken. I did not know that I was shot until my soul went to eternity."

At that point, according to Mrs. Sutton, Jimmie's apparition began to recede, but before vanishing he implored his mother, "Mamma, don't lose your mind because you have got to clear my name."

Lieutenant Sutton's phantom proved to be an unusually persistent one, reappearing often to provide his mother with fresh details of his murder. On one of his visits, his mother related, the phantom told how his attackers had bandaged his head, trying to hide what they had done. "My face was all beaten up and discolored and my forehead broken and a lump under my left jaw," he said. And the apparition named his chief assailant: "Utley managed and directed the whole affair." The apparition, still wrapped in the overcoat, kept looking for something and spoke of being unable to find a shoulder epaulet, apparently torn loose in the fight: "It's my shoulder knot that I can't find."

Soon the entire Sutton household seemed infected by the psychic presence. The dead Lieutenant's sister, Daisy, reported a dream in which a mysterious arm held a photograph before her. A voice told her, "There is the picture of the man who was most interested in directing the fight that killed Jimmie."

*Temple University founder Russell H. Conwell thought at first that his visions of his deceased wife, Sarah, were "a delusion of age." But the apparition, when it was tested, seemed to know things that he did not. Conwell said later that the implications of the case "are of the deepest significance to religious thought."*

Later, when the family received a photograph of the Lieutenant with a group of his fellow officers, Daisy was shocked to see the face of the man she had seen in her dream. It belonged to a Lieutenant Utley, the man the apparition had named to Sutton's mother.

Other details that seemed to corroborate the Suttons' psychic impressions began to emerge. When Lieutenant Sutton's effects were returned to the family, it was discovered that his watch crystal had been shattered, just as the apparition claimed. In addition, the shoulder epaulet that customarily adorned his uniform could not be located.

Driven on by persistent appearances of the phantom, the Suttons continued to probe their son's death. Soon, weaknesses in the official story and inconsistencies among eyewitness reports began to surface. Finally, in 1909, the Suttons had their son's body exhumed from Arlington National Cemetery. The examination confirmed many of the Suttons' suspicions. Although U.S. Navy doctors had testified at the inquest that Sutton's face was not disfigured, the body showed that he had received repeated blows to the forehead and that a pronounced lump had formed under his chin, exactly as the apparition itself had described.

Since there was never enough evidence to indict Lieutenant Utley or anyone else, the case of Jimmie Sutton's death may never be completely resolved. Yet it was Mrs. Sutton's psychical experiences that called the official suicide finding into question, and her evidence, received wholly through these channels, remains the most damaging to the initial ruling of the inquest.

As psychical researchers increasingly focus their attention on the issue of survival of the soul, two groups are emerging—the believers, or survivalists, and the disbelievers, or antisurvivalists. The antisurvivalists would explain away the alleged Sutton encounter as a matter of hallucinatory wish fulfillment combined with information gleaned through ESP. They would hold that in her grief, Rosa Sutton constructed the apparitional drama to provide an alternative to her son's reported suicide. Survivalists would counter by asking how she could possibly have obtained the wealth of information on her son's injuries—information that was only verified after his body was exhumed and the medical cover-up revealed. The answer to that, argue the antisurvivalists, is that Mrs. Sutton may have been able to reconstruct the scene and the injuries through clairvoyant or telepathic contact with living persons who were present at the time of her son's death. In other words, by gathering extrasensory impressions from living people, not her dead son, she may have been able to project a credible apparition of her son in his final crisis.

This scenario covers most of the facts in the case without confronting the survival issue. But survivalists find the argument thoroughly unconvincing. For one thing, Mrs. Sutton was not the only member of the family to have reported psychical experiences involving the dead lieutenant. Daisy, the sister, also received powerful impressions from an alleged apparition acting on behalf of her brother, and these impressions as well were later borne out by the facts. It is highly unlikely, say the survivalists, that two members of the Sutton family would be blessed with such strong telepathic powers.

Then there is the matter of motive, which always looms large in any assessment of apparitional experiences. Mrs. Sutton's motivation—an unwillingness to accept that her son's death was a suicide—was unquestionably a powerful one. But was it as urgent as Lieutenant Sutton's need to make known the facts of his brutal murder? Most likely it was not, contend the survivalists.

The question of survival of the soul has perhaps never been examined more closely than in the work of the parapsychologist Karlis Osis, from 1962 to 1975 the director of research at the American Society for Psychical Research. His methods reflect the careful standards of many modern psychical studies. One case that Osis investigated in 1983 gives a particularly clear illustration of his step-by-step methods and the conclusions they enable him to draw.

A thirty-six-year-old businessman named Leslie, as he is called in Osis's account, was piloting a small airplane across the southern United States when—at an altitude of 3,000 feet—he lost control of his craft and crashed to earth. He died instantly. His death was all the more devastating for the family in that Leslie's eighteen-month-old son, Ricky, had drowned only a year and a half earlier. Leslie's mother, Marge, was particularly distraught over the double loss.

A distant relative of Leslie's by marriage—called Constance in the Osis account—felt that she had experienced a premonition of the disaster. In a dream the day before Leslie's fatal crash, she had seen a plane spiraling down toward her. The fact that Leslie's death followed this vision left a profound impression on Constance, so much so that she was moved to attempt to contact him.

Holding a picture of Leslie in front of her, Constance spoke aloud as though he were sitting in the same room with her. "It would be a nice gesture," she said, "if you would go and find your little boy who drowned a year ago and take him by the hand and appear to your mother so that she will know that you are not dead, just separated from your body. And if she saw her little grandson with you, she would be more comforted." Constance repeated these words several times during the next two days, though at no time did she sense that Leslie or Ricky was present in the same room with her.

Two days after Constance first made her strange plea to the spirit world, Leslie's mother, Marge, awakened in the middle of the night to a disturbance in her room. "There he was," she later told Osis, "Leslie, with the baby, and he was holding the baby's hand .... They were at the foot of the bed. They looked at each other. I was wide awake then. They were content; they were happy that they found each other, that they were together now. And they were letting me know that it is so; I got that feeling."

Marge said that Leslie and the baby had appeared completely lifelike. "They were solid. There was like grayness around, like a gray cloud, ... mist in the whole room .... But they were solid, both of them." The experience was so riveting that everything else faded out. Marge explained that she lived in an area of heavy traffic and considerable noise. But when Leslie and Ricky appeared, there was "not one sound then, all was excluded at that moment, everything, as though the world had stood still. And there was nobody but us three in the world." The experience lasted about fifteen seconds, according to Marge. Then "they got smaller into the distance and faded out."

Marge maintained that she had never before undergone any sort of psychic encounter and had previously had no belief in an afterlife. In fact, she said later, "If someone else had told me about an experience like I had, I would think that person belongs in an institution." Marge, moreover, said she knew nothing of Constance's plea to Leslie's spirit. Nor was she aware that several hours earlier Leslie and Ricky had reportedly appeared briefly to Leslie's six-year-old niece, Jennifer, a child whom Constance had never met nor even been aware of.

This astonishing report of a dual appearance proved to be of particular interest to Osis. Within a year of Leslie's crash, Osis had gathered every available fact of the incident through interviews, psychological tests, and research into the family's history.

He entered the case as a scientist might, with no preconceptions—though critics have observed that he seems not to have considered the possibility of fraud or hoax. He assessed the mass of data he and his assistants had collected in terms of three psychical theories: the survival-of-personality model, which assumes that in an apparitional experience there is active participation by the agents, Leslie and Ricky in this case; the survival-of-fragments model, which holds that only fragments of thought or images generated in life survive death; and the super-ESP model, which attributes apparitional experiences to the powers of the living, in this instance Constance, Marge, and Jennifer.

Of the survival and ESP theories, Osis maintained that they "are perennials in the sense that they have successfully endured 100 years of critical evaluations and even passionate onslaughts." And while they may seem to be contradictory ideas, noted Osis, both have their merits in

# Phantom Friends

"I first saw them framed in the doorway; they were strange to me, as were all children." So wrote Eileen Garrett *(above)* of the three spirit companions who came to her in early childhood, departing when she entered her teens. The sensitive Irish girl, later to become famous as a medium, claimed that she met the two little girls and a boy on the County Meath farm where she grew up at the turn of the century. The visitors became her soul mates, she said, sustaining her through a lonely youth. But they were not like other children. For one thing, they communicated through some form of telepathy. Nor did they reveal their names or their origins. When the Irish girl asked to follow them home at the end of a day of play, "they shuddered and said 'No.' "

The adults on the farm never saw the children, and believed them to be mere imaginary playmates. But Garrett would insist that she did not invent her visitors. "I never doubted the reality of 'My Children' or the fact that we spoke in ways that no grown-up understood. I touched them and found that they were soft and warm, even as I. There was one way in which they differed from other people. I saw the form of ordinary humans surrounded by a nimbus of light, but the form of 'The Children' consisted entirely of this light."

Some students of spirit lore believe that the children represented a kind of visitation called companion, or counselor, ghosts—spirits whose mission seems to be friendship or guidance. In some cases, as in Garrett's, the companions are said to linger for years. In others, the spirits visit only once or twice and are never seen again. For instance, one eighteen-year-old girl, whose grandfather had always helped her with homework, said that his ghost paid her a visit six months after his death as she was puzzling over her lessons: "At about 3 A.M. my grandfather came through the outside wall of my bedroom, in a luminous circle of grey light, his head and shoulders clearly visible, and talked to me. Next day I found I could understand my problem."

A number of adventurers have also reported the presence of a guiding spirit, usually unseen, which sustained them in extremity. Explorer Ernest Shackleton, who led an epic three-man trek across the mountains of Antarctica in 1917, wrote, "I know that during that long march of thirty-six hours over the unnamed mountains and glaciers of South Georgia it often seemed to me that we were four, not three. And Worsley and Crean [Shackleton's companions] had the same idea." For Shackleton, the invisible presence, even if imagined, provided a very real support.

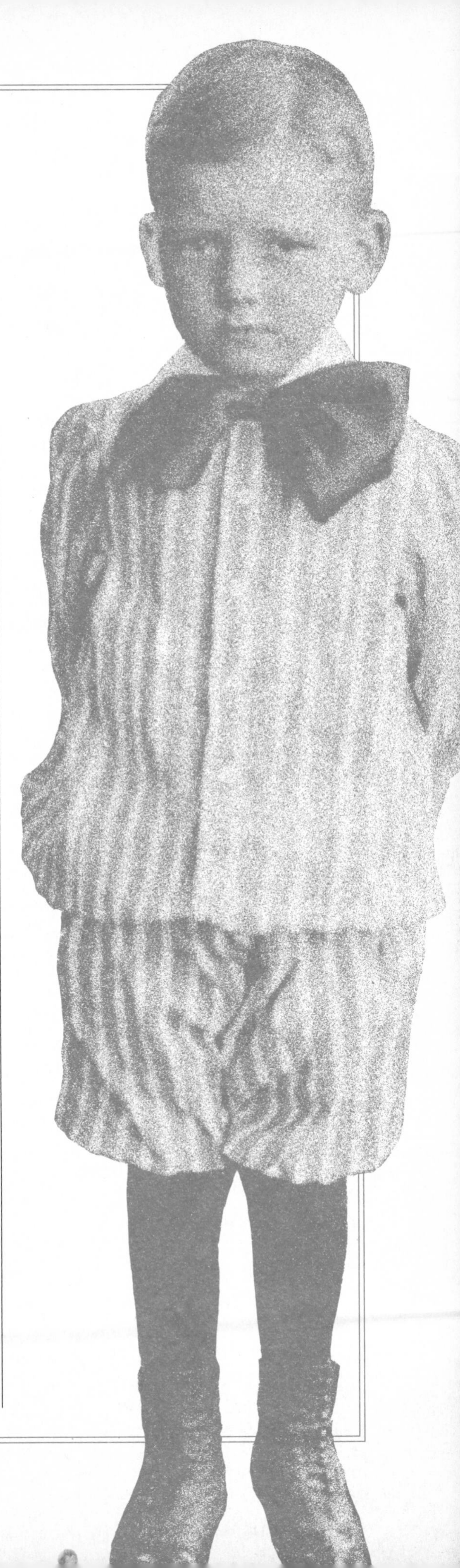

explaining some types of psychic encounters. It is always a good idea, the parapsychologist wrote, to "keep both forks of the road open."

In his analysis of the theories, Osis began by assuming that in the case of Constance and Leslie, where a living person made a request of a dead person, some sort of telepathic communication would have had to occur for any of the three models to be considered. He quickly disposed of the fragment-survival theory by finding "any satisfactory telepathic link" between fragments of a soul and the living "difficult to conceive." To Osis, that left the survival-of-personality and super-ESP models; either Leslie's and Ricky's personalities had answered Constance's plea by communicating with the living, or Constance, Marge, and Jennifer had engaged in some sort of complex telepathic round summoning up images of the deceased.

In examining the super-ESP hypothesis, Osis concluded that despite the fact that it at first appeared to offer a reasonable explanation, the theory became strained when one fully realized "the complexity and extent to which ESP would have had to have been operating. That hypothesis would assume that the personalities of Leslie and Ricky did not exist in any form after death. Therefore, figuratively speaking, Constance would have dialed a telephone number that was disconnected, and so the operator (presumably her unconscious) rerouted the call to Marge, about whom Constance was concerned."

But this rerouted call, Osis continued, "would have had to overcome three obstacles known to be detrimental to ESP: 1) the state of severe emotional stress experienced by the percipient, Marge; 2) the . . . attitude of disbelief in survival held by Marge; 3) the vagueness of the relationship between agent (Constance) and percipient (Marge), who had not seen one another for 13 years." Osis found the super-ESP hypothesis further weakened by the fact that Jennifer, the second percipient, was of no concern to Constance, particularly since she did not even know of the child's existence.

All in all, Osis found the super-ESP hypothesis quite unlikely. On the other hand, he found considerable merit in the survival-of-personality idea. He was impressed, for one thing, by the great similarity, or "correspondence," as he put it, between Constance's request for Leslie to soothe Marge's grief and the actual appearance, not only to Marge but to Jennifer as well. Wrote Osis: "The survival-of-personality model does well in explaining the nearly exact congruence between Constance's request to Leslie and the two apparitional experiences. This is so because it assumes a coordinator of these events, that is, the personality of Leslie." (Though Constance and Jennifer were totally unacquainted, Leslie knew everyone involved.)

One thing that did not quite fit the survival-of-personality model was the fact that the alleged apparition of Leslie and Ricky first appeared to Jennifer and not the requested target, Marge. Osis suggested, "Within the framework of the survival model, one could speculate that it was easier for Leslie to reach a believing little girl . . . than to contact his strongly disbelieving mother, who was stricken with grief and despair."

Osis concluded: "Let us remember that we operate in the domain of a very young science in which many uncertainties still prevail. One case alone cannot decide the survival issue. Different scholars will interpret the data differently, each according to their own belief systems. The manifest characteristics of this case certainly do not support the notion that apparitions are static images void of consciousness; something much more powerful and purposeful seems to be indicated."

Whether or not this is so—and skeptics would insist that all reports of apparitions are the results of hallucination, hoax, or fraud—the research will doubtless continue. Millions throughout the world will persist in the belief that the dead live on in spirit form, and some will concur with the optimistic pronouncement of the psychical researcher Julian Burton. "Perhaps eventually the sensational and scary nature of 'campfire'-type ghost stories will give way to the realization that experiencing visits from the dead may be a commonplace function of day-to-day living."

Ghost stories are staples of virtually every culture in the world, but nowhere are they more numerous or better loved—or more venomous—than in Japan. Purposeful and passionate, Japanese phantoms cling to earth with malicious intent, usually to wring vengeance from those who wronged them in life. Next to them, the vaporous wailers and cautionary Dickensian chain rattlers of the West pale in comparison.

Japanese notions about ghosts are rooted in the ancient animistic religion of Shinto, which holds that human spirits are destined for an eternal world. But there is also an in-between realm between earth and eternity, a nebulous, ambiguous half-world from which unhappy spirits can return to plague the living. Thus Shinto is replete with rituals aimed at appeasing the spirits of the dead. With the advent of Buddhism in Japan, the malignity of ghosts was augmented by the suggestion that they hatched their plots not in some postlife twilight but in hell itself.

Whether purgatorial or hell born, Japanese ghosts have moved from the realm of religion and folklore into that of art to remarkable effect. Many have found their way into literature and from there to drama. Ghosts have been frequent protagonists in kabuki theater, the repository of Japanese popular culture, since its incep-

*Protesting oppressive feudalism in nineteenth-century Japan, a play about the ghost of a martyred peasant gained great popularity. The drama, based on fact, had as its villain one Lord Hotta Kōzuke, who levied burdensome taxes on his subjects in the province of Soma. Though law forbade it, the farmers decided to seek relief from the Shogun, the country's military dictator. A brave village chieftain named Sakura Sōgorō delivered their petition. The Shogun promptly returned it to Hotta Kōzuke, whereupon the evil lord forced Sōgorō and his wife to watch while their three sons were beheaded. Then he had the parents crucified. From the cross, Sōgorō vowed that his ghost would return to haunt his family's tormentor. At right, a print by Utagawa Kuniyoshi depicts the haunting of Hotta Kōzuke. He cowers at the center while the shades of Sōgorō and his wife swoop toward him from the upper corners of the picture. A second Sōgorō ghost attacks from behind. Sōgorō has even managed to change Hotta Kōzuke's servants into demons, a talent seldom ascribed to Western ghosts.*

織越大領 政知
一勇斎
國芳画

*A powerful eighteenth-century samurai named Aoyama Tessan harbored a passion for one of his servants, the beautiful Okiku. When she rejected his overtures, Tessan plotted to trap her.*

*He owned ten valuable Dutch plates, which he had entrusted to Okiku's care. After hiding one of them, he demanded she produce all ten. Okiku could find only nine, of course, though she counted again and again. Near despair, she nevertheless refused Tessan's offer to forget the incident if she would become his mistress. Furious, Tessan killed her and threw her body down a well.*

*Thereafter, Okiku's ghost rose from the well each night and slowly began to count. When she reached nine, she wailed and then disappeared.*

*Tortured by the constant reminder of his guilt, Tessan sought help from a neighbor, who promised to exorcise the well. One night he hid beside it and waited until Okiku rose and counted to nine, whereupon he shouted "ten!" and she vanished, never to return.*

*Tsukioka Yoshitoshi's 1889 print memorializes the forlorn maid, whose story, told with many variations, is among the two or three best-loved of all Japanese ghost tales.*

*Women appear in Japanese ghost stories far more often than men, but not usually in a flattering light. They are either victims whose spirits return for vengeance to the living or evildoers whose sins invite hauntings.*

*In the latter category is the faithless wife of one Kohada Koheiji. Her lover killed Koheiji and later married the murdered man's widow. But thereafter the perfidious pair were tormented by Koheiji's ghost, and they eventually died violently.*

*Koheiji's spirit first appeared in a work called A Weird Story of Revenge in the Swamp of Asaka, written by Santō Kyōden and published in 1803. It was quickly adapted by playwrights of the kabuki theater and became a popular theme for prints. At right, a version by Shunkōsai Hokuei shows Koheiji's skeletal shade peering over a mosquito netting as his doomed wife recites in vain an incantation to protect her from haunting. The fiendish, bloodshot eyes bulging from the naked skull make the ghost seem particularly frightful and malign. The flames licking along the skull are thought to symbolize the betrayed husband's smoldering desire for revenge.*

# The Haunted Lovers

*Vengeance is again the theme in the story of Matahachi and Kikuno, a domestic drama of betrayal and murder.*

*A man named Igano Kanemitsu was having an affair with his older brother's widow—an especially egregious liaison, since the widow had become a nun. When the dead brother's mistress, Kikuno, and one of her servants, Matahachi, discovered the affair, Kanemitsu had both of them murdered. But the pair came back to haunt the illicit lovers, both to end the affair and to avenge their own deaths.*

*Double suicide by lovers was a frequent plot in kabuki plays; their supposed fate was to return as ghosts, eternally tied at the waist for transgressing the dictates of duty and dishonoring themselves and their families. Kikuno and Matahachi were not lovers, nor did they kill themselves, but Utagawa Kunisada's artistic rendering of their story follows the convention of linking the male and female haunters as they return to threaten Kanemitsu and his paramour. In other ways as well, the spectral appearances are typical of traditions regarding Japanese ghosts: They are bloody and disheveled, and their skin has a bluish tinge.*

相馬の古内裏に
将門の姫君瀧夜叉
妖術を以て味方を集
むる大宅太郎光國
瀧夜叉姫
大宅太郎光國
一勇齋國芳画
一勇齋國芳画

# The Sorceress Princess

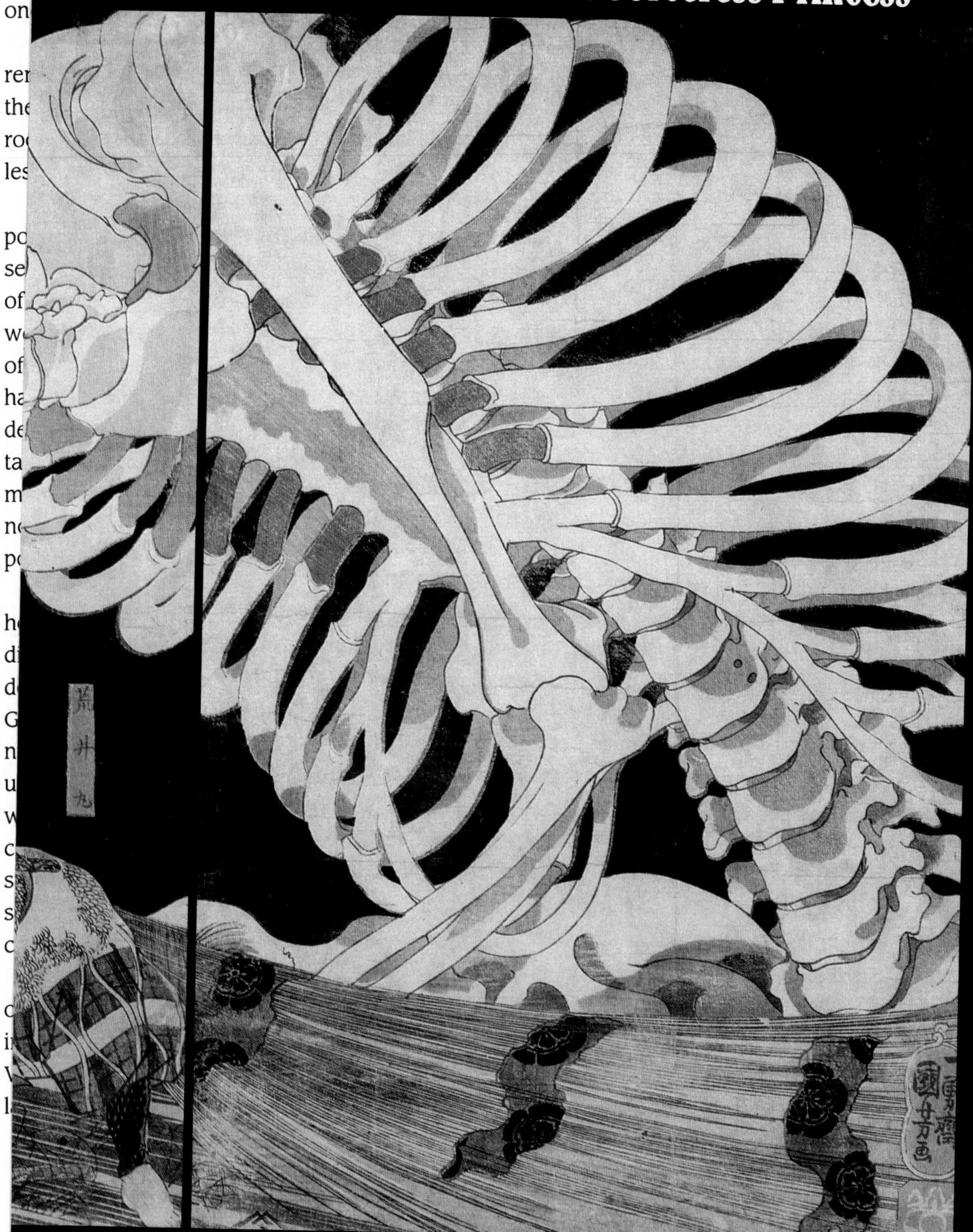

*One of the most popular nineteenth-century kabuki plays recounted the legend of Princess Takiyasha's unsuccessful attempt to conquer her enemies by enlisting the aid of ghosts. The princess was the daughter of a noble who died in the year 940 during the course of an abortive rebellion against his liege lord. After her father's death, Takiyasha became a nun. Later, however, she and her stepbrother met the spirit of a sorcerer frog, who used witchcraft to help them plot a rebellion against her dead father's rivals. The siblings closeted themselves inside their father's palace to formulate their plans. But an enemy warrior, Mitsukuni, discovered the cabal and eventually laid waste the palace and defeated both the humans and their supernatural allies.*

*A Kuniyoshi print shows the confrontation between Takiyasha and Mitsukuni. The princess is casting a spell that summons up a huge ghost in the form of a skeleton. The apparition gropes its way toward Mitsukuni over a fallen bamboo blind, while the warrior puts the rebellious stepbrother to the sword.*

# The Evil Pope's Double

A Pinturicchio fresco in the Vatican shows Pope Alexander VI in a pious attitude—a misleading pose at best. Even by the licentious standards of Renaissance Italy, Alexander, born Roderigo Borgia, was a master of depravity and his pontificate a reign of murder, incest, duplicity, and greed.

The seventy-three-year-old pope died in 1503, probably from malaria. But given his reputation, his demise evoked more sinister interpretations, including one with supernatural overtones.

This legend has it that Alexander was the victim of a plot that backfired. As the story goes, the pope, having passed an edict claiming estates of all deceased cardinals for the Holy See, planned to kill a certain wealthy cardinal for his money. Thus Alexander invited himself and his ferocious son Cesare to the proposed victim's home for dinner. The Borgias were providing the wine, which was poisoned.

Walking to the banquet, Alexander realized he had forgotten an amulet that he believed made him invulnerable to poison. He sent a companion, a Cardinal Caraffa, to retrieve it.

Entering the Pope's bedroom, the cardinal was met by an extraordinary sight. A black-draped bier lighted by torches rose in the center of the room. Atop it lay a corpse, its features all too familiar to Caraffa. They belonged to Alexander VI, the man he had just left.

At the banquet, meanwhile, a mix-up in the wine caused the pope to drink his own poison. A few days later, he was dead—just as Caraffa had foreseen.

the benches. Knowing Carne Rasch was seriously ill, Parker was surprised to find him present and, as he later told a newspaper, gestured to the man, saying, "I hope you are feeling better."

Carne Rasch made no acknowledgment but merely sat there impassively. A moment later, when Parker looked again, the man was gone. Parker hurried to the lobby to search for his friend, but no one had seen him pass by. Another colleague, Sir Arthur Hayter, reported later that he too had noticed Carne Rasch sitting on the bench and had called this to the attention of a third member.

Told afterward of the apparition, Carne Rasch expressed no doubt at all that his spirit had gone to the debate, since he had been very eager to attend. His family, however, perhaps out of fear that the phantom signaled an ill fate for Carne Rasch, was appalled to hear that his fetch had reportedly visited the Commons. (On returning to his normal parliamentary duties, Carne Rasch himself was a bit annoyed to find that colleagues sometimes poked and prodded him to make sure that he was appearing in the flesh.)

The idea of the fetch (also called waft or fye in England) goes back to pagan times and is found in most cultures. The human double has long been thought to be a manifestation of the soul and, therefore, a precious entity. The ancient Greeks believed it was dangerous to see one's reflection—or double—in a pool of water lest the soul be captured there. The Zulus of Africa still cling to this belief, and they also hold that one's shadow represents the soul as well and that it might be lost or injured by carelessness. And many societies have long-standing superstitions about the breaking of mirrors—which, it is feared, will trap the soul and lead to death.

Although early Christians turned the double into the attractive notion of a kindly guardian angel, the more primitive aspects of the double persisted in folklore, where its appearance was viewed by many as ominous. Tradition held that the double's materialization usually meant the soul had escaped the body and death was imminent. The seventeenth-century English folklorist John Aubrey wrote that Lady Diana Rich, daughter of the Earl of Holland, saw "her own apparition, habit and everything" while strolling about her father's garden in Kensington. A month later she died of smallpox. Lady Diana's sister was also said to have seen her double just before her death. Queen Elizabeth I saw her fetch not long before her death in 1603: According to one chronicler, it was lying in bed looking "pallid, shrivelled and wan." And about a month before he drowned in a boating accident, the poet Shelley saw his fetch.

But the appearance of a double was not always considered to be an omen of impending death. A double could supposedly wander off on its own mysterious business, particularly when one was asleep—leading to the notion that it was not a good idea to wake anyone up too suddenly, lest the double, or soul, be locked out. And the double could, in some cases, be deliberately sent forth. Cotton Mather chronicled some of the grimmer versions of such sallies in his 1692 account of the heyday of witchcraft in the New England colonies. Witches would send their fetches out in the night to "ride" people in their beds—hence the term *hagridden*—paralyzing them and rendering them speechless.

For the pioneering psychoanalyst Sigmund Freud, who explored the human double in a 1919 paper titled "The 'Uncanny,' " the double represented not only the soul, but in some cases the conscience as well. Freud reasoned that the idea of the human double began in the far reaches of human prehistory as a hedge against confronting the death of the ego, or self—a denial of mortality. This notion of an immortal counterpart arises, he wrote, from childish or primitive self-love. When this stage—in a life or in a civilization—is left behind, idea of the double persists, but as "the ghastly harbinger of death."

Freud was not the first to try to unravel the mystery of the human double. Systematic efforts to investigate and explain apparitions had begun with the founding in 1882 of the Society for Psychical Research (SPR). In particular, the publication in 1886 of the landmark book *Phantasms of the Living* launched modern inquiry into the phenomenon.

*A very real Sir Gilbert Parker (right) is shown in the House of Commons, where, in 1905, he supposedly saw a double of his colleague, Sir Frederick Carne Rasch (left). Two other members of Parliament also said they saw Carne Rasch that same day, even though he was ill at the time, absent from the Commons, and home in bed—in the flesh if not in spirit.*

Many of the 701 apparitions of the living chronicled in this work were "crisis accounts," in which spirits would appear to loved ones at or near the time of their deaths or during a particularly stressful moment in their lives. But many other encounters occurred during times of calm. A typical case of this sort was reported in 1860 by the Reverend W. Mountford of Boston.

Mountford had been in England, visiting the home of friends. One afternoon, at about four o'clock, he saw through a window his host's brother and sister-in-law approaching along the road in a horse-drawn open carriage. Reverend Mountford informed the host, who, with his wife, came to the window and made small talk about the impending arrival. But the couple in the carriage drove straight past the house and out of sight. The host was amazed by this event: His brother and sister-in-law had passed by without stopping in, "a thing they never did in their lives before."

A few minutes later, the host's niece arrived, looking flustered. Just before four o'clock, the young woman explained, she had left her parents at home by the fire to walk over to her uncle's house. But on the way, her parents had driven past her on the road without looking at her or saying a word. About ten minutes later, Reverend Mountford, looking through the window again, saw the pair coming down the road once more, still in the open carriage. The host was even more perplexed since there was no way, given the configuration of the roads, that the couple could have driven by the house the first time and then have returned to approach again from the original direction. He ran outside and asked them about it, but they assured him that this was the only time they had been on the road that day. Furthermore, they said, they had come directly from home.

"Then you mean to say," the host asked, "that really you did not pass by here ten or fifteen minutes ago?" "No," came the reply, "at that time, probably, we were just coming out of the yard."

As in the case of Emilie Sagée, the doubles had seemed to appear to several percipients at the same time,

without the apparents' knowledge and for no particular reason. The SPR researchers speculated that in this instance, the host's brother had unwittingly sent a telepathic message to the percipients about the planned visit—a message that included the sender's wife. Presumably, the percipients had then proceeded to construct a common hallucinatory tableau. The fact that the doubles were accompanied by a horse and carriage—indeed even the fact that doubles always seemed to appear fully clothed—would seem to reinforce the theory of telepathic projection. For if the double was some form of the soul, as many people thought, and not a figure conjured in the mind of the percipient, then why, when it wandered away from the body, would it take along clothes, or for that matter a means of transportation?

*Pragmatic though she was, England's Queen Elizabeth I saw her doppelgänger shortly before she died. The pale and wizened fetch was lying on the queen's bed.*

The case of Mrs. E. H. Elgee of Bedford, England, seemed to bolster this notion. Mrs. Elgee was on her way to India in November 1864, when she and a traveler in her charge, whom she referred to in her account as "Miss D.," were forced to stay over in Cairo. The hotel was undistinguished, and their room was large and gloomy, with only a minimum of furniture and two beds placed in the middle of the room. As the women settled in for the night, Mrs. Elgee locked the door to the room and put the key under her pillow. In case some would-be intruder had a duplicate key, the women put a chair against the door and placed Mrs. Elgee's traveling bag on it. Then they went to bed.

At dawn, Mrs. Elgee awoke "with the impression that somebody had called me" and found herself looking at "an old and very valued friend whom I knew to be in England." In the early light streaming through an open window, Mrs. Elgee noted her friend's clothing in detail, even the onyx shirt studs he always wore. The figure approached a step or two, then pointed at the other bed where Miss D., sitting up, was staring at him in terror. The figure retreated and, as Mrs. Elgee recounted, "seemed to sink" through the door.

The woman's next recollection was that the sun was brightly shining. Unsure whether she had been dreaming or had actually seen "a visitant from another world—the bodily presence of my friend being utterly impossible," Mrs. Elgee resolved to say nothing of her experience with her friend to Miss D. in order to find out if her companion had also seen the apparition.

As it turned out, Miss D. remarked upon waking that the chair and traveling bag set against the door had not worked as an alarm. "That man who was in the room this morning must have got in somehow," she said. Miss D.'s description perfectly fit Mrs. Elgee's friend, and when questioned, Miss D. maintained she had never seen the man before. Mrs. Elgee, her observations thus confirmed by Miss D., assumed that her friend's phantom appearance somehow signified that he had died. Several years later, Mrs. Elgee found to her surprise her friend was alive, and she determined that at the time the apparition appeared, he had been offered a job about which he had mixed feelings; the man had stayed up late worrying about it, wishing that Mrs. Elgee were present to advise him.

Some have seen this as a near-classic case, in which the desire of Mrs. Elgee's friend to see her prompted a telepathic visit by his apparition. Of course, there is ample room for doubt: The event was recalled some twenty years after its alleged occurrence, and human memory is often faulty. Even the fact that the episode belonged to the most reliable category of apparition cases—the collective cases, such as Reverend Mountford's, where more than one person witnesses the same apparition—did not make it easier to explain. Collective cases would require a telepathic communication from the apparent to a percipient, and then a further transfer from that percipient to another. But the SPR researchers felt that the sheer number of such incidents, reported by people who seemed otherwise to be upstanding members of society, made the overall phenomenon not only believable but something that called out for serious investigation and explanation.

In 1923, Eleanor Sidgwick, the wife of one of the SPR's chief founders, published an updated supplement to *Phantasms of the Living,* in which she included many more recent accounts. One aspect of the phenomenon to which all investigators remained alert was the so-called veridical apparition—encounters during which the percipient learns something from the apparition that he or she could not otherwise have known. (This is especially common in crisis accounts, where one person may claim to learn of another's death and even the details of their demise.)

One such instance reported by Eleanor Sidgwick was the case of a boarding school student named J. P. Challacombe. It occurred on a March night in 1898. The boy had gone to bed at about 10:00 but was restless and could not sleep. He began thinking of home and his mother, and before long he heard someone coming up the stairs. His first thought was that it was his mother, and then suddenly she appeared to him. She was wearing "a black dress that I had never seen before, and had on her pink shawl and gold chain, and as she came into the room her shoes creaked." The student was not frightened, but felt that something held him back from getting up to greet her. But the mother soon approached her son's bed and kissed him. "I tried to kiss her but could not," the boy said, "then she disappeared and seemed to vanish in a mist."

The boy had no way of knowing it, but at the time of his vision, his mother had just returned from a walk. "My dress Jack had never seen," she testified, "and I am not in the habit of wearing my chain outside my dress. As for the boots, they were a pair I had not worn for years, because they were in the habit of creaking."

Mrs. Sidgwick felt obliged to list this account as "ambiguous," since the mother and son had, after all, had time to discuss the matter before reporting it. But, Sidgwick wrote, not only did the apparition convey information as to the apparent's "actual condition at the moment," it was also a rare instance of a realistic apparition affecting three senses—sight, hearing, and touch. Jack's utterly vivid and three-dimensional impression raised still more questions about the human mind and its powers. Yet the SPR researchers stuck fast to their theory of telepathic hallucination, characterizing as "remembered or represented sensation" the realistic sensory data reported in hallucinations such as young Challacombe's.

At the time of the SPR study, researchers made no attempts to reproduce apparitional encounters in a controlled environment, so the SPR's theories could not be explored fully. But there was a category of alleged apparitions of the living that drew special attention from the early researchers. These cases—in which the apparent consciously tried to appear as an apparition to a particular percipient—were designated "experimental," although they could more precisely be called deliberate.

For example, one December evening in 1882, at about 9:30, a Mr. S.H.B. reportedly went into a room alone at home and, thinking of a lady of his acquaintance, determined "so strongly to fix my mind upon the interior of a house at Kew . . . in which resided Miss V. and her two sisters, that I seemed to be actually in the house.'' S.H.B. went into something akin to a hypnotic trance for about thirty minutes, and then wrote down his intention on a piece of paper. Later, when he went to bed that night, he once again determined to produce a spiritual presence in Miss V.'s home—this time willing himself to appear in her bedroom at the hour of midnight.

The following day, S.H.B. visited the house at Kew without mentioning his attempts the previous evening at what can be presumed to be a bit of innocent Victorian voyeurism. There he encountered one of Miss V.'s sisters, who told him, without prompting, that she had seen him twice the night before—once at about 9:30, walking through a corridor in the house, and again at midnight, in the bedroom she was sharing with Miss V. The sister, claiming to have been wide awake, described seeing S.H.B.'s apparition enter the room and take her long hair into his hand. The phantom next took the woman's hand in his, stared at it intently, and then disappeared—whereupon the sister woke Miss V. to tell her about the encounter.

After hearing the sister's account, which was confirmed by Miss V., S.H.B. took from his pocket his jottings from the previous evening. He showed the paper to the two ladies—who were, it was said, ''much astonished although incredulous.''

Taking note in 1943 of this and other deliberate cases, G. N. M. Tyrrell, a psychical investigator and SPR member, reported that there were records of at least sixteen cases in which an apparent sought to appear to a particular percipient or in a certain place. In most instances, the attempt was successful on the first try, suggesting a repeatable ex-

***In 1771, the German poet Johann Wolfgang von Goethe had a prescient vision of his doppelgänger. While traveling to Drusenheim, he imagined seeing himself, in unfamiliar clothes, riding in the opposite direction. Eight years later he found himself on the same road, wearing the very clothes he had imagined.***

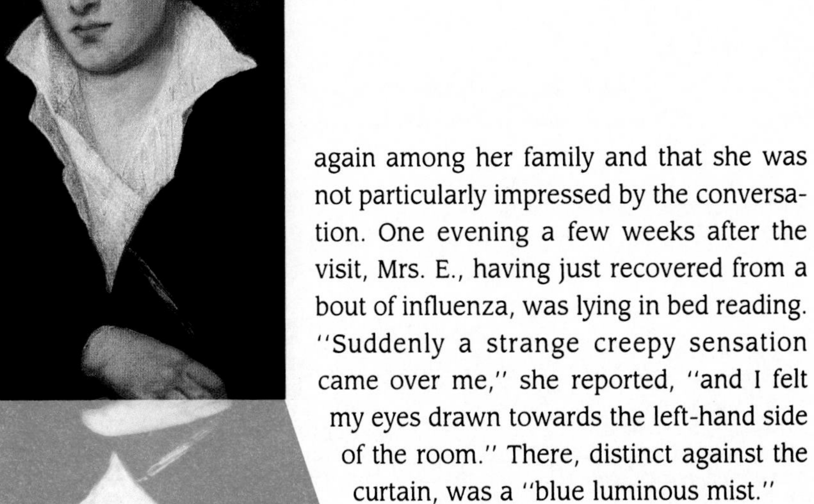

Percy Bysshe Shelley allegedly saw his wraith in 1882 while boarding a small boat that later foundered, drowning the young poet.

periment that for some reason had "been ignored by investigators." For if apparitions could be manufactured at will, Tyrrell wrote, then testing equipment, such as cameras, could be used to record the phantoms and to prove once and for all that they are a reality.

Yet the attempts still were not made. Contemporary investigators of such capabilities had moved away by then from hard-to-verify personal accounts and were seeking to study, in laboratories, all forms of extrasensory perception—including telepathy, clairvoyance, and precognition—using strict scientific methods. The investigators were hoping to show that certain people were especially adept at telepathic projection, much as SPR founder Frederic Myers had claimed in his 1903 book, titled *Human Personality and Its Survival of Bodily Death*. In this posthumously published work, Myers, believing that the soul survived death and returned to communicate with the living, reiterated the theory of telepathic hallucinations. He examined cases of deliberate apparition projections and concluded that some people simply had a particular talent for letting their souls go. Certainly the accounts that were available to him were suggestive, and few were more so than that of a Mr. Rose.

One Sunday evening in the early 1890s, Rose was visiting the family of Mrs. E. when he was asked what he had been doing lately. Replied the guest: "My last effort has been trying to send my 'spook' here." Mrs. E. asked him to explain, but insisted later that the subject was not discussed again among her family and that she was not particularly impressed by the conversation. One evening a few weeks after the visit, Mrs. E., having just recovered from a bout of influenza, was lying in bed reading. "Suddenly a strange creepy sensation came over me," she reported, "and I felt my eyes drawn towards the left-hand side of the room." There, distinct against the curtain, was a "blue luminous mist."

The terrified woman could not take her eyes off the strange sight but decided against calling out to her son, in case he would think she was ill. Summoning her courage, Mrs. E. turned away from the mist and resumed reading her book. In due course, "the dread and feeling of awe" came again, and she saw the blue mist steadily creeping up the side of the bed toward her. She held her book in front of her as if to shield her face and was fighting off panic when "suddenly, as if with a jerk, above the top of my book came the brow and eyes of Mr. Rose." All fear left her at that moment, and in a reaction that was considerably unlike that of Miss V.'s sister, who had not seemed to mind the apparitional invasion of her bedroom, Mrs. E. dropped her book "with an exclamation not complimentary." In an instant, she reported, "mist and face were gone."

The next day, Rose paid a visit to the house. Mrs. E., before revealing her experiences from the previous night, asked him about his activities the prior evening. "I went to my room early," he said, "and concentrated all my thoughts in trying to send my astral body here." Mrs. E. confirmed that his efforts had been successful, then extracted a prom-

# Lifelines for the Dead

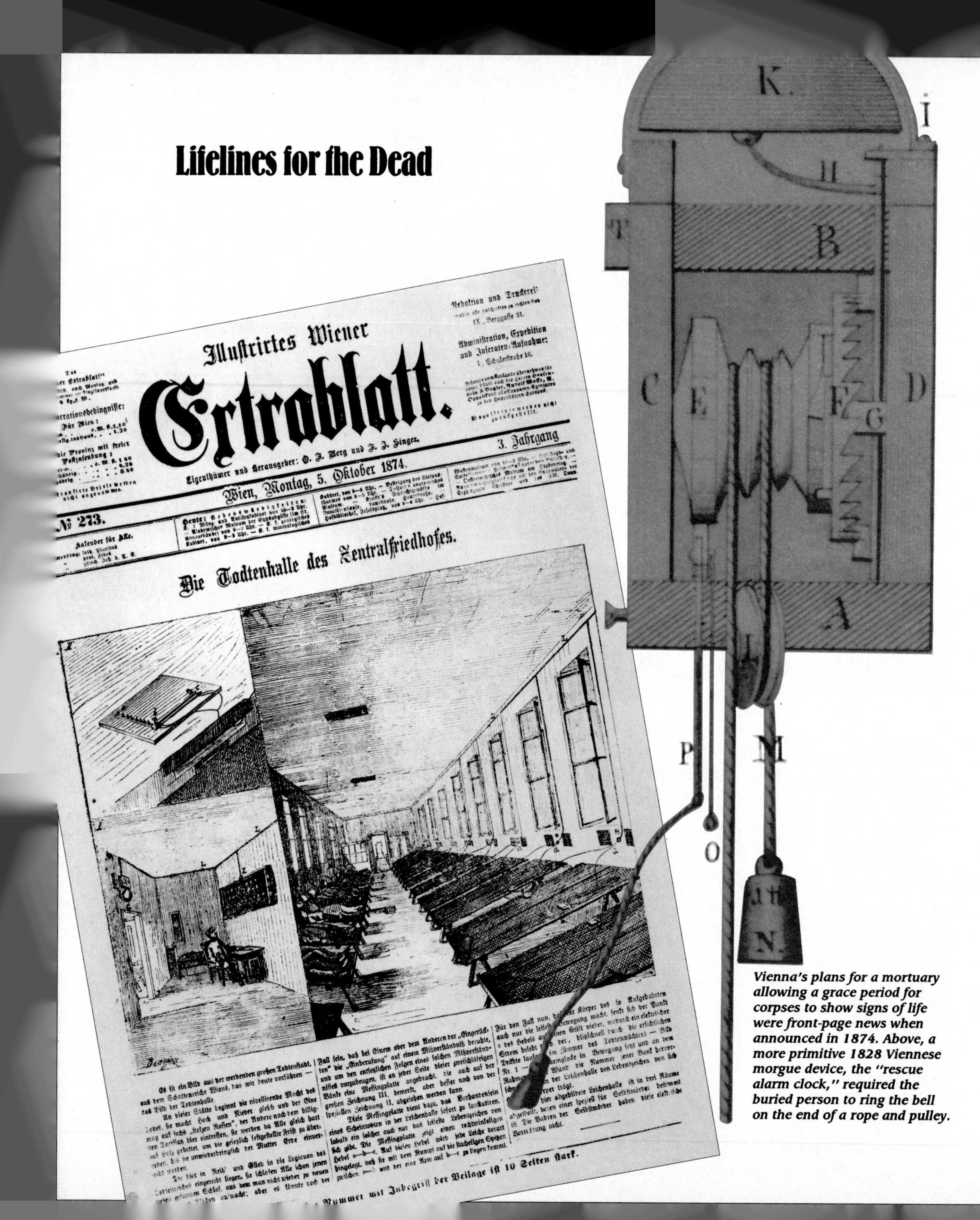

Illustrirtes Wiener

Extrablatt.

Eigenthümer und Herausgeber: O. F. Berg und F. J. Singer.

Wien, Montag, 5. Oktober 1874.

3. Jahrgang

№ 273.

Redaktion und Druckerei: IX., Berggasse 31.

Administration, Expedition und Inseraten-Aufnahme: I., Schulerstraße 16.

Die Todtenhalle des Zentralfriedhofes.

Nummer mit Inbegriff der Beilage ist 10 Seiten stark.



*Vienna's plans for a mortuary allowing a grace period for corpses to show signs of life were front-page news when announced in 1874. Above, a more primitive 1828 Viennese morgue device, the "rescue alarm clock," required the buried person to ring the bell on the end of a rope and pulley.*

In ghost lore, apparitions are usually perceived as humans who have died and returned as spirits. Perhaps the ineffable nature of death itself helped fuel these tales. But what if some individuals who were thought to have died and come back had not, in fact, ever died in the first place? Modern medicine may pose new questions about defining death; in earlier days, however, there was a more basic problem—how to recognize it.

"The difference between the end of a weak life, and the commencement of death, is so small, and the uncertainty of the signs of the latter is so well established," London surgeon G. A. Walker wrote in 1839, "that we can scarcely suppose undertakers capable of distinguishing an apparent from a real death." Even if the old-time morticians had possessed the skill to detect faint signs of life, they often lacked time to look for them. In cases of such raging contagions as typhoid and cholera, infected bodies were often shoved underground quickly to protect the living. And in the absence of modern embalming, the line that is now clearly crossed with the bloodletting on a mortuary table did not exist.

So it was that in Europe and even in America, gruesome tales of premature burials arose—most apocryphal, but some probably true. Dr. Franz Hartmann, a physician during the late 1800s, estimated that in Germany alone there were thousands of premature interments every year.

Fear of being buried alive became common, even finding its way into literature. Edgar Allan Poe, for instance, was almost obsessive about it. It figures in several of his short stories, including "The Fall of the House of Usher" and "The Premature Burial."

Poe was not the only one consumed by the horror of waking up in one's grave. For years before his death in 1875, Hans Christian Andersen, the Danish author of fairy tales, never went to bed without leaving a note on his bed table saying, "am merely in suspended animation." A few days before he died, he instructed a friend to open his veins after his presumptive demise, just to make sure.

The great Russian writer Nikolai Gogol detailed all sorts of precautions to prevent his premature burial—and in his case the fear may have been more than neurotic morbidity. A few years after his death in 1852, the government set about to move his remains to a more prestigious site. When Gogol's coffin was opened, his body, having somehow turned itself, was lying face down.

Fear of such a dreadful fate created a market, and entrepreneurs were quick to fill it. There was brisk traffic in coffins that were fitted with contraptions allowing the too-hastily buried to signal their dilemma to those above ground. One featured a ground-level bell to be rung from inside the coffin. Another contained a pneumatically operated signaling device that could be triggered by the movements of an erstwhile corpse.

But the largest safeguard against premature burial was found in Vienna. There, in 1874, plans were announced for a new morgue, a temporary structure for use pending completion of a vast new necropolis for the burgeoning city. It offered the very latest in scientific protection. Corpses were laid out on double couches equipped with metal plates. The plates had two small levers to detect the slightest movement in a body and send an electrical signal to ring a bell in the morgue's central room. A numbering system corresponding to the bells allowed an official on watch there to tell which body had moved and rush to its aid. The only couches not thus equipped were those for suicides, who, city fathers reasoned, clearly wished to stay dead.

Although the morgue was abandoned after the completion of the new cemetery complex, the popular bell system was incorporated into the new facilities. It is not recorded in either place that any presumed cadaver ever rang one of the bells.

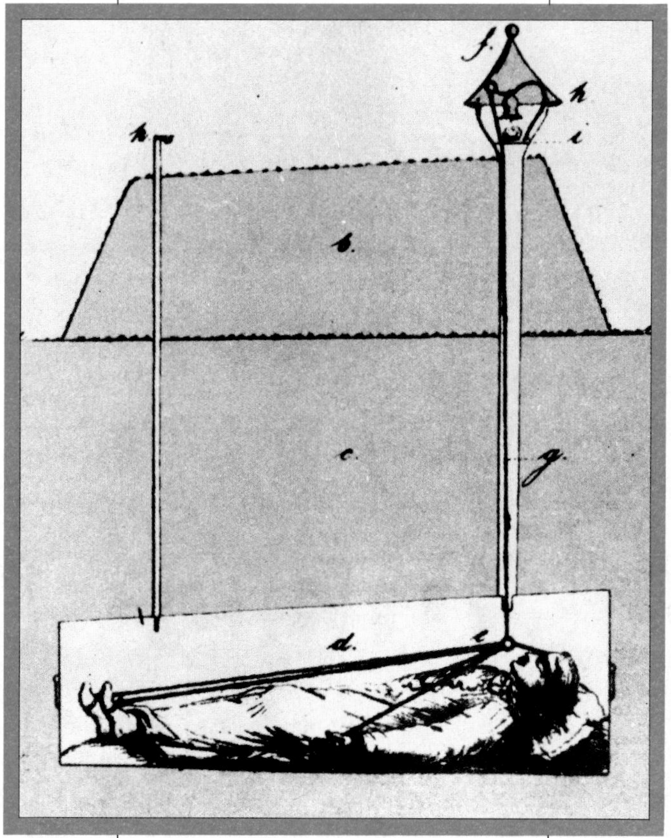

***With this mechanical arrangement, a victim of premature burial could ring a bell by moving either hands or feet.***

ise from Rose that he would not experiment on her again, as it made her "nervous."

Rarely, it seems, do percipients take offense at deliberate invasions by apparitions, however astonished they may be. One case of serene acceptance of an apparitional visit involved a colleague of Harvard University psychology professor William James. The gentleman, James reported, was "an able and respected professor" and felt comfortable confiding in the open-minded philosopher and psychologist, but wished to remain otherwise anonymous lest his "experiment" seem frivolous and disgraceful to other, more conservative colleagues.

The professor had been seeing a lady friend, "A.," quite often, and the two shared an interest in the theory of the existence of astral (or spirit) bodies. One evening in late 1883 or early 1884, the professor sought to project his astral body into A.'s presence. He sat in the dark by an open window that faced in the direction of her house, about half a mile away. "I . . . tried as hard as I could to wish myself into the presence of A.," the professor recalled, and he remained in "that state of wishing for about ten minutes. Nothing abnormal in the way of feelings happened."

The next day, A. reported that during the previous evening, while having dinner with someone, she had seen the professor peering through the door. She told her companion, whose back was toward the door; the friend reasoned that if the professor were really there, he would come into the room. The apparition retreated, unseen by the friend; nevertheless, both apparent and percipient were convinced of the reality of the event.

As such talents began to be investigated in the laboratory, reports from the field diminished. Indeed, the paucity in the twentieth century of such phenomena gave rise to considerable doubts that there was anything to them at all. But then an incident known as the Landau case occurred, raising several old and unresolved questions.

In 1955, during the month of September, Lucian Landau, a member of the Society for Psychical Research, was living in London, as was his fiancée, Eileen. Landau was ill, though medical tests had turned up nothing in particular, and Eileen had moved to a bedroom next to Landau's in order to take care of him. One morning she claimed that she had come into his room the night before—without her physical body—to take his pulse.

Landau asked Eileen to repeat this performance the next night and handed her his diary, requesting that she bring it with her when she came again. At dawn the next morning, as Landau later recounted, he awoke suddenly and saw Eileen standing by the door; she was wearing a nightdress, and her face was nearly white. The figure—which was perfectly opaque—began to glide out of the door onto the landing. Landau followed and watched the pale woman move toward the open door of Eileen's room; through the doorway he could see Eileen sleeping, the bedclothes moving rhythmically as she breathed. The figure approached the bed where she lay, then vanished.

Back in his room, Landau spotted next to his bed a small rubber toy dog that Eileen typically kept on her bureau. Later in the morning, the young woman reported that she had gone to the desk to collect the diary but couldn't bring herself to pick it up. Instead she picked up the toy dog, and she recalled carrying it into Landau's room and seeing him asleep. She remembered feeling very tired and wanting to go back to bed but did not recall returning to her room. Some researchers believe this incident to be especially remarkable because it showed that an apparition could transport a solid object—proof, they maintain, that something besides a mere hallucination was at work.

The case also pointed to another aspect of such events—the troublesome distinction between apparitions of the living and what are called out-of-body experiences. In an apparitional encounter, the apparent is typically unaware of its fetch, even if its appearance is a result of a deliberate effort: Emilie Sagée knew that her double was on the move only by the reactions of the young women around her. On the other hand, out-of-body experiences normally are said to involve a transfer of consciousness from the apparent to its astral form. This etheric body becomes the conscious one, often seeing other people and even the physical body it left behind. And in such situations, others present do not see the astral body at all. In the Landau case, the apparition seemed to be the site of Eileen's consciousness, but Landau saw both the apparition and the physical body. This, of course, raised again the old question of whether apparitions were subjective experiences living in the mind of the percipient or had a real and objective existence of their own.

One student of the paranormal who had not been convinced that apparitions of the living could be simple, or even complex, telepathic hallucinations was A. Campbell Holms. In his 1925 book, *The Facts of Psychic Science and Philosophy: Collated and Discussed,* Holms examined numerous reports of telepathy and clairvoyance, and he concluded that if an agent thought fixedly of a triangle, as opposed to other available shapes before him, the intended percipient would see the triangle. By the same token, he wrote, if the agent focused his mind on the percipient, logic suggests that the percipient would see what was in the apparent's mind—that is, he would see an apparition of himself, not of the apparent. To Holms's mind, this argued for the objective reality of the phantoms that appeared to so many percipients. In other words, according to Holms, there was some being that actually left the body.

In a somewhat different vein, G. N. M. Tyrrell cited one case from Düsseldorf, Germany, in about 1820, in which the figure in an alleged apparition was not that of the agent, explaining that this "might be expected when one realizes that an apparition is only a mode of conveying a message, which may consist of anything." In this admittedly rare case, a government assessor named H. M. Wesermann evidently had a hobby of trying to make his own apparition appear to various people. One night, though, he concentrated on projecting the apparition of a woman who had died five years earlier into the bedroom of an acquaintance identified only as "Lieutenant ____n." Wesermann was unaware that the lieutenant was not at home, but was sharing a suite of rooms elsewhere with a fellow officer. The two men were about to retire for the night when the door to the kitchen reportedly opened and the figure of a woman, very pale and dressed in white, entered. She paused, greeted each man with a wave, and then went out through the same door. The men followed her "to discover whether there were any deception, but found nothing."

In this intriguing case, Wesermann seemingly not only projected the apparition of another apparent—the woman—to the lieutenant and his friend, but the apparition appeared to have sought the young officer out at his unexpected lodgings. According to Tyrrell, this case confirmed his theory that an agent was capable of producing a thought pattern that could make itself evident to others and could act independently of the agent. At the same time, he raised the question of whether the ghost of a dead person is really the thought pattern of some telepathically adept living person.

Tyrrell also cited a case that allegedly occurred one evening while a husband and wife were entertaining another couple for dinner. All four were sitting around the dining room table when the host saw an apparition of his wife standing by the sideboard. "It is Sarah," he said, and all looked up to see the figure of their hostess wearing a light muslin dress that, Sarah reported, was unlike anything in her wardrobe. Then the vision disappeared.

It could be argued that, in such instances, one person sees a hallucination and, by making note of it, influences others by the power of suggestion. But if this were true, Tyrrell pointed out, "the world would become peopled with apparitions to such an extent that one would never be sure who were the living people."

The case of Sarah, as with several other examples, was also one where the presumed agent and the percipient were the same person—a matter of seeing one's own double. Psychical researchers Celia Green and Charles McCreery have called such encounters "autophany." This is distinct from "autoscopy," which refers to allegedly seeing one's own body from outside, as in out-of-body experienc-

# The Great Ghost Maker

Two passions of Victorian England were science and spiritualism, and nowhere were they better merged than in the person of John Henry Pepper.

Pepper was an analytical chemist who in 1852 became director of London's Royal Polytechnic Institution. This establishment worked to disseminate scientific knowledge to the public, a task Pepper thought was best accomplished by making science fun. He especially liked explaining complex concepts and devices by using optical apparatus that produced grand dioramas and dissolving views. So it was that he came to devise his Ghost Show, which enchanted audiences in Canada, Australia, and the U.S., as well as his native Britain.

The Ghost Show allowed an audience the illusion of interacting with phantoms on stage, and its effect relied on the same principle that lets you see successive reflections of yourself in a train window while riding at night. The "ghost" was an actor positioned in front of the stage and below it, but concealed from the audience's view. Hidden beneath the stage, a projectionist illuminated the actor, whose image reflected in a mirror and from there onto a large glass pane stationed obliquely in front of the onlookers and more or less invisible to them. A variety of grisly apparitional effects were possible, most seeming to menace either the patrons or other actors.

Famed as a preeminent showman of science, Pepper never pretended his ghosts were anything but illusions—a refreshing contrast to fraudulent mediums, abounding at the time, who insisted their shades were real.

*John Henry Pepper did it with mirrors.*

*An engraving shows how Pepper made his magic. His first ghostly production was a dramatization of a Charles Dickens Christmas story. It was presented at the Royal Polytechnic Institution on Christmas, 1862.*

es. Autophany is often associated with illness or exhaustion, which may account for the notion of seeing one's double as an omen of impending death. In their 1975 book, titled *Apparitions,* Green and McCreery cite the example of a woman in Brisbane, Australia, who ran a boardinghouse for fifteen young men. One night, utterly exhausted from a day of grueling housework, she sat down with some of the boarders to watch television. Before long, the woman reported, she saw her body floating above her for a few moments, "all white and transparent and lying in the same pose as I did myself. I stared wonderingly and then suddenly it wasn't there. I looked around at my companions but they didn't seem to have noticed anything."

The percipient's state of mind, as well as his or her physical health, may also play a role in autophany, as illustrated by the story of a woman who reportedly saw her double one evening in March 1978, after she had put her children to bed. She had been working at her sewing machine, she recalled, when she heard one of the children tossing restlessly. Upon entering the child's room, she saw "the image of myself stooping over the end of the bed, in a dress which I had not been wearing for some time." The figure appeared to be grieving, although the woman herself was "neither specially sad nor specially excited" that night. Three months before, however, one of her children had died, and it occurred to the woman "that after death my child was laid across the foot of my bed, and I may have stood in that attitude then. The dress, too, was the one I was wearing at the time."

While ill health or psychological suffering, such as this woman may have been feeling, might explain some autophany experiences, Green and McCreery report that the majority of such sightings occur when people are feeling perfectly well. The two researchers cite the story of a man who claimed he was "in excellent fettle" at the time of his alleged encounter. A widower who had lived alone for more than ten years, he awoke one night in late March 1960 "with a convulsive jerk all over, conscious of a nearby presence." In the moonlight, he saw a figure dressed in pajamalike clothing, standing near his bed. He naturally assumed that it was an intruder—probably a burglar—and sat up suddenly with his right fist drawn back. Then, the man reported, "I let fly as hard as I could, but just before contacting I glanced up to the face and saw it was myself! Too late to stop, the fist went through the body." At that, the phantom figure instantly vanished.

One might well be suspicious of a story about an apparition in which both the percipient and the apparent are the same and there are no witnesses. But there is a category of accounts—a type of veridical apparition—in which people have reported receiving useful information from their own double. The most celebrated such case may be that of the French author Guy de Maupassant. In 1885, he was at work on a short story and was experiencing that familiar hazard of the trade, writer's block.

According to Maupassant, a figure appeared at the door to the writer's study, walked across the room, and sat down opposite him. Maupassant was amazed that anyone had gotten into his study and was even more amazed when the intruder proceeded to dictate the words of the author's story. At that moment, he discovered that the intruder was no stranger, but his own double. Before long the apparition disappeared, leaving Maupassant to continue the tale as it had been dictated—the story of an invisible evil spirit that lives within a man, yet independently of him. The being cannot be escaped, and it tortures its host to madness. The story, titled "The Horla," was, some feel, a harbinger of Maupassant's subsequent madness and death.

A more mundane but equally notable case reportedly took place in Holland in 1944. A repairman was asked by a manufacturing company to fix an adding machine. He visited the plant and began work on the machine, a brand unfamiliar to him. In due course he got the apparatus in working order—except that the machine could not accurately add in the hundreds. The repairman was baffled.

One night, however, he was awakened in his bedroom and saw the machine on a table, next to a lamp that was

# Phantoms of the Mind

However ghosts are defined in the West, in the East they are sometimes believed to be creations of the human mind, just as real, and just as illusory, as all the rest of creation.

This is especially true in Tibet, as Frenchwoman Alexandra David-Neel discovered. An opera singer and journalist in her youth, the venturesome David-Neel later became fascinated by Tibet and spent years assimilating and writing about its culture and religion.

She was especially intrigued by Buddhist mysticism's notion of the *tulpa*—a magical entity created by concentrated thought. The tulpa springs from the mind of its creator, but it is visible to others and may have a will of its own. Creating a tulpa is said to require a disciplined mind, one that is given to seclusion, meditation, and the mastery of certain rituals. Envisioning the being one wants to create is central to the process.

David-Neel's book *Magic and Mystery in Tibet* tells how, over a period of several months, she brought forth the tulpa of a fat, jolly monk. He became a kind of amiable houseguest, but gradually gained autonomy and changed from pet to pest. He acquired what his maker called "a vaguely mocking, sly, malignant look." Eventually, she decided to reverse the creation process and destroy the thought form. She was successful, but only after six months of arduous concentration.

***Alexandra David-Neel, disguised as a peasant, was the first Western woman to visit Lhasa. She died in 1969 at the age of 100.***

giving off a bright light. He saw himself, fully dressed, lean over the machine and, with his left hand, remove a little triangular part; the figure pinched one end of the part with pliers and put it back in the machine. The next morning the man returned to the plant, mimicked the action of his double the night before, and repaired the adding machine.

An even more helpful double was reported by Gordon Barrows, who was later to become the managing editor of the trade journal, *World Petroleum.* After being discharged from the United States Army in 1946, Barrows returned home to see his parents in Wyoming and then went to college at the University of Wyoming at Laramie. While at school that winter, Barrows decided he would like to use a jeep that he had purchased earlier at a sale of surplus army equipment. During spring break, he went home to pick up the jeep, then set off for Laramie. Because of the bitterly cold weather, Barrows was bundled up in parka, mittens, and boots. He had driven through the day and into the night when a blizzard overtook him. Cars were stopped along the road, but he kept on going in the jeep.

As he topped a hill and started down into a canyon, he saw a man walking along on the side of the road. Barrows stopped to offer the man a ride, and when the figure walked within range of the jeep's headlights, Barrows had a start: The man looked just like him and was wearing a light Tank Corps jacket, like the one he had worn during the war. "Somehow," Barrows recalled, "this odd coincidence seemed the most natural thing in the world." As the figure approached he said to Barrows, "You look sleepy. Want me to drive?" In fact, the young man was exhausted; he had been driving for eighteen hours and was numb with the cold. Barrows went to sleep, and the other man took the wheel. The next thing Barrows recalled was waking up in silence. The engine was not running, and the man was sitting motionless in the driver's seat. They were at the end of the canyon, and Laramie was a straight shot ahead on level ground, forty miles away.

The passenger got out of the jeep, refusing a ride into Laramie. When Barrows thanked him, he simply replied, "You're welcome," and started walking back into the canyon. Barrows recalled that at the time the events all seemed natural, "like in a dream in which preposterous things seem ordinary." But it was not a dream. And Barrows knows that if any human being had been walking in that snow-swept canyon, he could not have survived more than an hour or two. Barrows believed his own life was saved by his double.

Another type of apparition of the living is said to serve a specific function—that of alerting the percipient to the apparent's imminent arrival. Such a case was reported to the SPR by Dr. George Wyld in 1882; the incident concerned a close friend of his, Miss Jackson. The woman was accustomed to visiting the poor. Once, while making a round of visits, she had an overwhelming desire to be home, warming herself at the kitchen stove. Precisely at that moment, two housemaids in her kitchen saw the doorknob turn and the door open. Miss Jackson then came in and went directly to the stove to warm her hands. The maids took note that on her hands she was wearing handsome green kid gloves. Then suddenly, the woman disappeared.

The astonished maids went to Miss Jackson's mother and told her every detail of the event, down to the gloves the woman had worn. The mother reasoned that since Miss Jackson did not have any green gloves, the appearance was surely imagined. Thirty minutes later, when Miss Jackson herself came home and went to the stove to warm her hands, she was in fact wearing green gloves.

Arrival cases, as they are called, occur with some frequency. In one reported instance, a man was startled to see his twin brother's figure appear in the room; it struck him "like a mild shock of electricity." The vision gradually disappeared, but only moments later the man's twin was actually tapping at the window; he had unexpectedly arrived for a visit. In another case, a major in the British army saw a superior officer enter a mess hall carrying some fishing tackle. The major went to look for the officer, but he was not there, and in fact, no one could recall having seen him for several hours. Shortly thereafter, the officer arrived at

***Guy de Maupassant thought a fetch helped him write "The Horla," a story of a man maddened by the notion of an invisible being usurping his life. Published in 1887, the tale probably reflected the writer's own encroaching insanity. Six years later he was dead.***

the barracks with his fishing gear in hand, dressed in precisely the same clothes that the major had seen him wearing. When asked if he had been in the mess hall about ten minutes before, the officer said no, he had just that moment returned from fishing.

Nowhere, it seems, are arrival cases more common than in Norway. There, the double is referred to as the *vardøgr* and has taken on the special role of forerunner. Thorstein Wereide, a professor at the University of Oslo and an early member of Norway's Society for Psychical Research, wrote in the 1950s that the vardøgr appears at one's destination when one is about to leave for that place, regardless of the distance or the time involved in the journey. And its appearance in Norway is usually auditory rather than visual. The percipient will hear the rattling of a key in the lock, overshoes being kicked off, the sounds of familiar footsteps. The vardøgr's appearances can become so regular that the percipient addresses the person, saying "Is it you or your vardøgr?"

In such situations, it is claimed, the percipient can sometimes put the phenomenon to practical use. This was reportedly done with a student at the University of Oslo, Wiers Jensen, who lived at a boardinghouse early in this century. His evening hours were irregular, making it difficult for the hostess to know when to prepare Jensen's evening meal; however, his vardøgr reportedly made regular appearances, and the hostess would know that it was time to start cooking. When Jensen arrived at the boardinghouse, his dinner was ready.

Professor Wereide himself claimed to have a vardøgr like Jensen's. His wife would often hear it—and occasionally see it—when Wereide was about to leave the university for the trip home. He believed his wife was particularly receptive, since he had not had such experiences before his marriage. In his opinion, projections of this kind were probably common throughout the world, but Norway had more people who were sensitive to them. The reason, he decided, was that for centuries the Norwegians had lived in remote areas of the countryside and in mountains where communications are especially difficult. "Nature," he wrote, "seems to have made use of 'supernatural' means to compensate for this isolation."

One might argue that such apparitions are what Frederic Myers called "expectation images"—projections of what the observer was hoping to see. But some researchers maintain that the supposed accuracy with which people have noted these forerunners, even when there is no particular schedule involved, suggests that there may be more to many arrival cases than mere wishful thinking.

Indeed, apparitions seem also to arise from precisely the opposite motivation: dread. Such was the celebrated case of "Ruth," an American woman living in England in the 1970s. Happily married and the mother of three, Ruth had begun seeing apparitions of her father, who was at that time living in the United States. These visions were extremely painful for Ruth, inasmuch as her father had severely abused her as a child. She would see his face superimposed over that of her husband. She would feel the bed move when he appeared and bumped against it with his legs. She could smell his perspiration. The frightful experiences were causing a strain on Ruth that began affecting her relationships with her husband and children; finally, the twenty-five-year-old woman put herself in the hands of a psychiatrist, Morton Schatzman.

A thorough physical examination, including tests of her sensory organs and brain function, ruled out any physical disorders. Following Schatzman's advice that she attempt to confront and conquer her apparitional enemy, Ruth learned, after months of therapy, to control her father's image to the extent that she could call it up or dismiss it at will. Further, at the doctor's suggestion, Ruth also tried to conjure up other people—friends and other relatives—and she demonstrated a remarkable ability to produce hallucinations of "reality." Schatzman eliminated any possibility that the apparitions might have an existence beyond Ruth's mind by carrying out a number of experiments. The woman claimed that if the apparitions she projected stood before her, they blocked her vision of the room beyond. By measuring her brain waves, Schatzman determined that when Ruth was hallucinating, the reaction of her brain to visual stimuli ceased—"as if something had actually blocked the stimuli." According to Schatzman, a beam of light would evoke a normal response from her retina, the light-sensitive surface at the back of the eye, but her brain did not pick up the signal.

Were Ruth's phantoms purely subjective? It would seem so. No one else saw her father's apparition when it appeared, for example. But the entities she saw were real enough to her to affect her brain waves. And during Schatzman's treatment, as Ruth became more and more comfortable with producing hallucinations, she claimed to have created her own double.

One of the most remarkable things about Ruth's story is that she was not only adept at consciously creating hallucinations but capable of producing them under laboratory conditions, that is, while she was wired to various measuring devices. In most cases, modern researchers into parapsychological phenomena have found that clinical conditions are inhibiting. In addition, most psychiatrists and others in the medical profession are likely to consider hallucinations to be a sign of possible mental illness, which tends to inhibit people from mentioning apparitional encounters—and largely removes these phenomena from the realm of clinical study.

The mystery cannot be removed by ignoring it, and apparitions of the living will continue to be reported. Recent surveys in places as diverse as Italy, Hong Kong, and the United States have indicated that those who believe in these things—and who maintain that they have experienced them—are generally among the young and well educated rather than the older and less educated, who would presumably be more suggestible or superstitious. Until science one day explains these events, they will continue to tantalize believers and anyone else who ponders the frontiers of consciousness.

# The Haunted Tower: Mortar

Conceived in conquest and emblematic of violent death, the Tower of London is one of the world's bloodiest historic sites—and also, some say, one of the most ghost ridden. Over the centuries, the Tower has variously been a fortress, a castle, a storehouse, an armory, even a zoo. But it is woven most tightly into British history as a prison and a killing ground, the site of innumerable hangings, burnings, drawings and quarterings, and beheadings. There, nobles met their deaths at royal whim, and even crowned heads were claimed by the executioner's ax.

The Tower site is old beyond reckoning. When William the Conqueror overcame the Saxons in the eleventh century, he found, still standing along the Thames, stretches of ancient Roman walls. Their location was attractive strategically, so William chose to build a fortress within their shelter. A rude military camp served well enough for a while, but in 1078 the king began erecting a vast stone edifice to serve as both fortress and palace. This was the White Tower, which still stands, little changed over the past 900 years, as a monument to Norman architecture. It formed the nucleus of the Tower of London, which is not a single building but an eighteen-acre compound of towers, yards, battlements, houses, and other structures.

Many of William's successors made changes in the Tower, improving its fortifications or

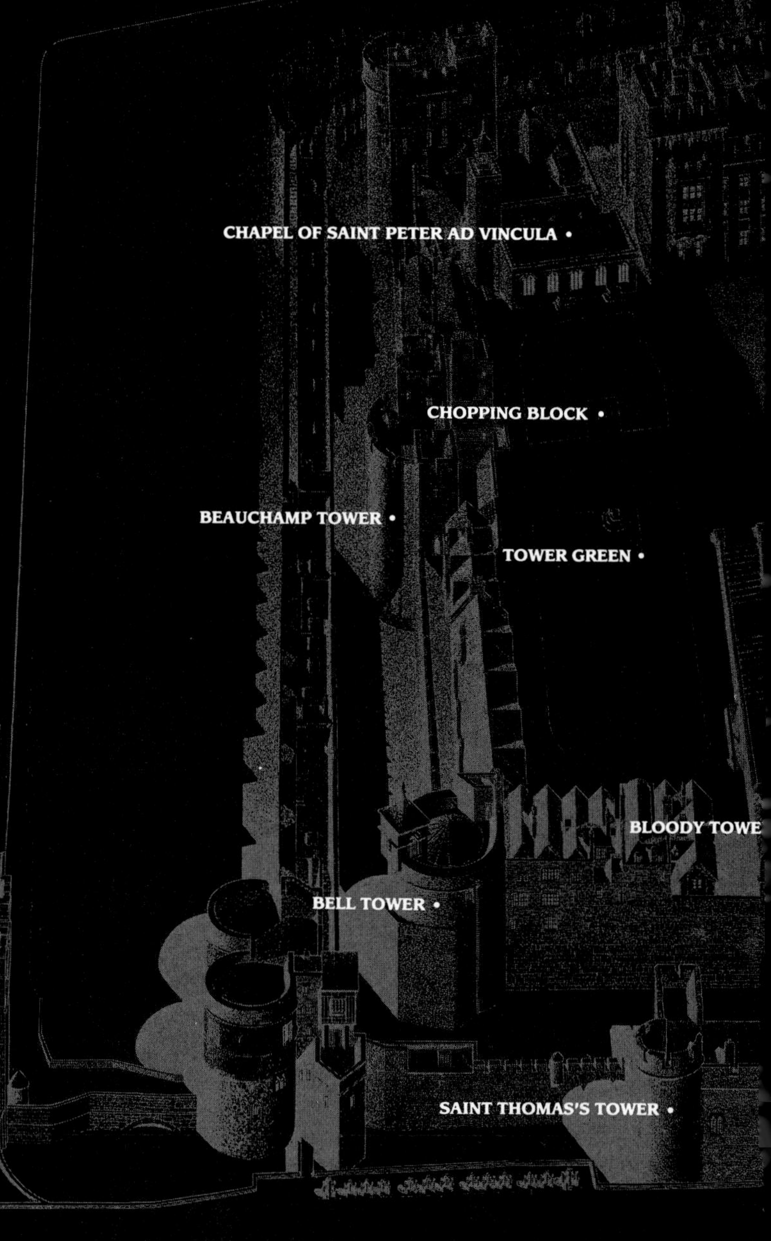

# and Misery, Stones and Blood

expanding its functions. In the thirteenth century, for instance, both Henry III and Edward I spent huge sums on building programs for the complex, some of which were designed to make the royal quarters more comfortable. But by the end of the sixteenth century, the Tower was no longer used as a royal residence, having become mainly a state prison and home to government offices. Eventually, its penal and bureaucratic functions defunct, the complex became what it is today: an imposing tourist attraction that houses, among other national treasures, the crown jewels.

The Tower of London bears testament to the grandeur of English history, and also to its periodic cruel perversity. Centuries of monarchical tinkering may have altered its structural details and lineaments, but the finest architectural revisions could not begin to expunge the Tower's notorious legacy of death or exorcise its bloody earth. Legend has it that the complex is haunted by the spirits of many of those inmates who suffered or died within its grim confines; some of their stories are presented on the following six pages. Evidence that such restless phantoms actually exist is nothing more than anecdotal, but the ghost stories persist, clinging tenaciously as London fog to the Tower's cold gray stones.

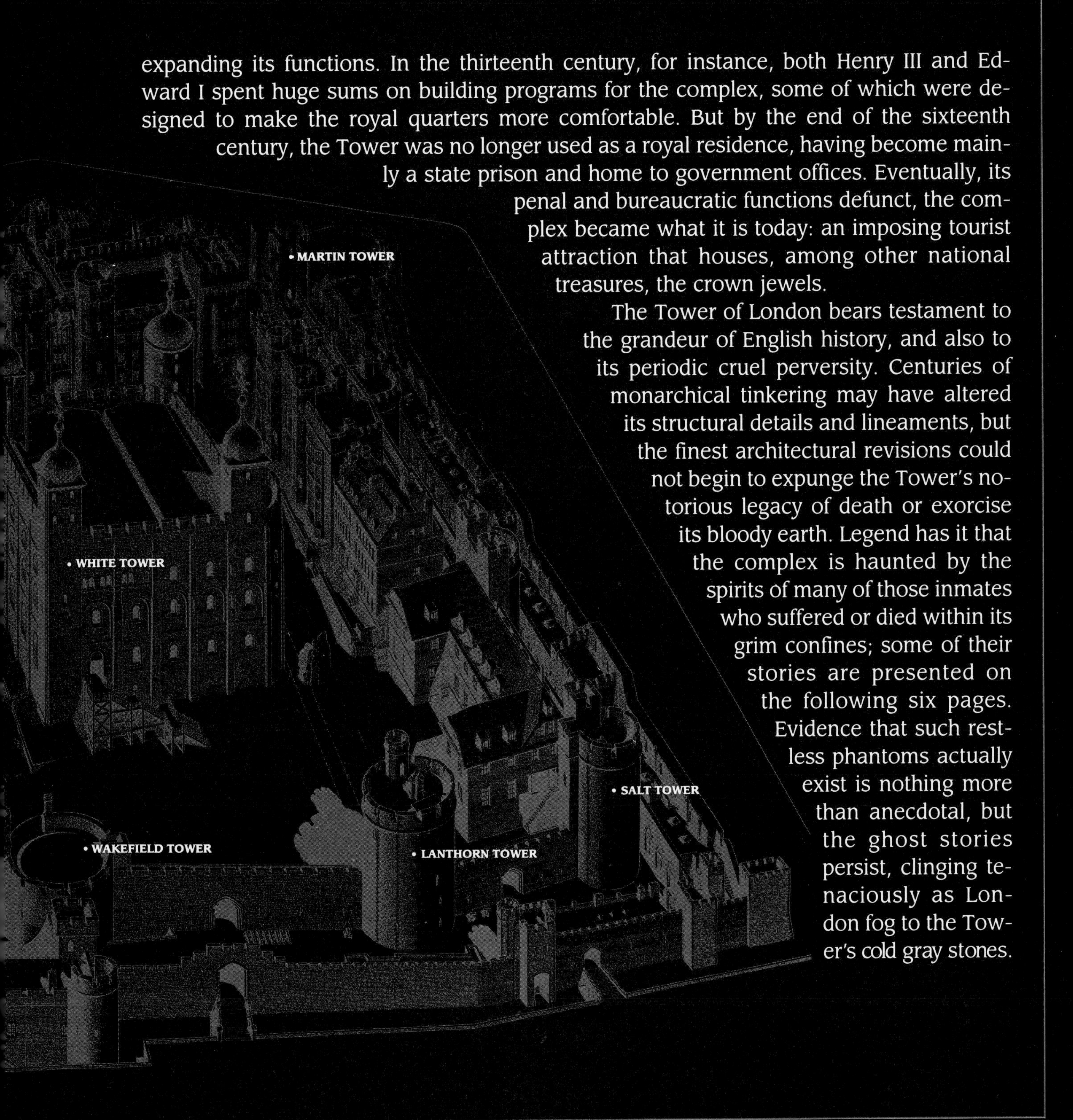

# Headless Men and a Murdered King

**The Unknown Victim.** Not all of the Tower's victims died within its precincts. Many were taken from imprisonment to Tower Hill, just outside the walled perimeter, to be hanged, beheaded, or otherwise dispatched. Usually their bodies were returned to the Tower grounds for burial. During World War II, a sentry on night patrol outside the Tower's main entrance was startled by an odd cortege approaching his post. Several men in old-fashioned uniforms bore a stretcher. Atop it lay a decapitated body, its head tucked between one of its arms and its torso. The group vanished only a few yards from the sentry. No identity was ascribed to the beheaded victim, but there were indications the sentry had somehow peered into history. In relating his vision, he accurately described uniforms worn by sheriff's men who, during the Middle Ages, returned corpses to the Tower for burial.

**The Little Princes.** On the death in 1483 of Edward IV, his twelve-year-old son ascended the throne as King Edward V, and the new king's younger brother, Richard, became Duke of York. Their guardian was their uncle, Richard, Duke of Gloucester, who coveted the throne himself. Gloucester contrived to have the children declared illegitimate; thereupon he took the crown as Richard III. The boys were confined to the Tower and there disappeared from history. No evidence ever came to light linking Richard to his nephews' departure. Indeed, he had no clear motive for harming them, since they were not a threat to his throne. Nevertheless, legend has it the boys were murdered on Richard's orders in the Bloody Tower, which probably derives its name from that presumed event. Ghosts of the boys, nightgown clad and hand in hand, have reportedly appeared near the Bloody Tower and elsewhere on Tower grounds.

**Thomas à Becket.** Becket was both chancellor and best friend to Henry II, but after Henry named him Archbishop of Canterbury, a rift developed. Henry had expected his long-time crony to side with him in his incessant bickering with the Roman Catholic Church. But Becket put his church before his king, and in 1170 Henry retaliated by having three assassins stab the archbishop to death in his own cathedral. The martyred Becket was canonized three years later, and Henry, bowing to Church demands, was forced to do penance for his old friend's murder. Although Becket did not die at the Tower, he apparently chose the site for vengeance. A new tower and watergate ordered built there by Henry's grandson, Henry III, neared completion twice, only to be destroyed—once by a storm and the second time for no apparent cause. A priest claimed that he had seen Becket's ghost battering the stonework with his cross.

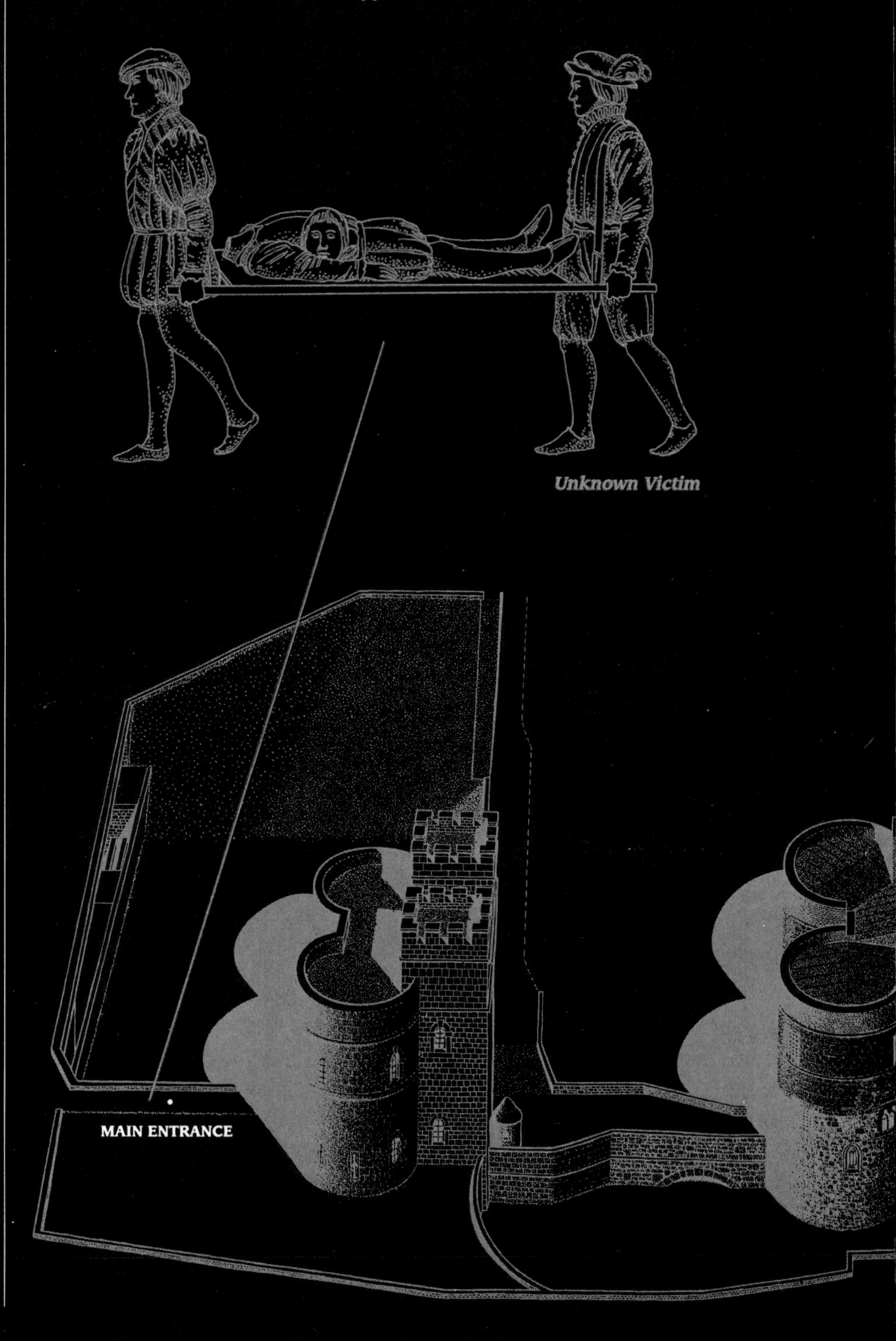


*Unknown Victim*

**Henry VI.** A pious but weak-willed monarch, Henry VI spent most of his reign buffeted by contending forces in the English civil strife known as the War of the Roses. The Lancastrian king eventually found himself imprisoned in the Tower as an opposing Yorkist took the throne to become Edward IV. On the night of May 21, 1471, Henry was stabbed to death, probably at Edward's behest, while praying in a small oratory in the Wakefield Tower. His ghost is said to have been seen sitting outside the oratory, his hands folded in prayer.

**The Cloaked Man.** One night in the late 1960s, a sentry who was patrolling the walls between the Wakefield and Lanthorn towers rushed into his guardroom, prickling with fear. "Man in cloak! Man in cloak!" was all he could gasp. But when he was calmer, he told how a cloaked figure had appeared from the shadows during his patrol. The sentry was about to challenge the anonymous intruder when he saw that it was headless.

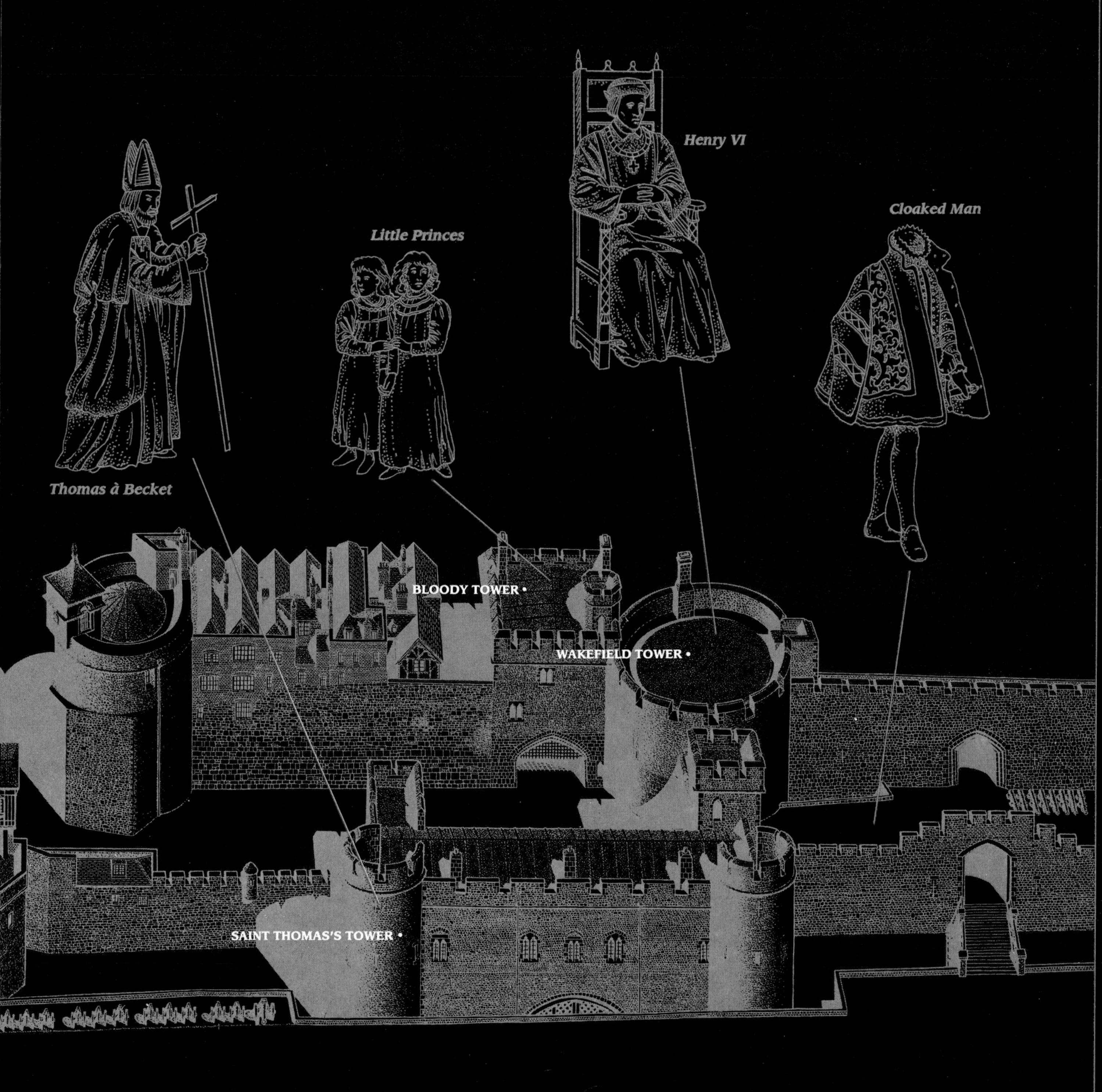

# A Grim Chase and a Beheaded Queen

**The Duke of Monmouth.** James Crofts was the illegitimate son of Charles II. His father, who had no lawful heir, acknowledged and adored young Jamie, and made him Duke of Monmouth. Charles was to be succeeded by his brother James, a Catholic and therefore unpopular in Protestant England. A movement arose to have Monmouth declared legitimate and a rightful heir, but Charles would not trifle with the succession, and his brother became King James II in 1685. After Monmouth made a futile try at asserting his own royal claim by force, James sent him to the Tower for treason. The young duke was beheaded the same year as James's ascension. A phantom in cavalier's garb, possibly Monmouth's ghost, supposedly has been seen moving along the battlements connecting the Bell and Beauchamp towers.

**The Countess of Salisbury.** The founding of the Tudor dynasty posed a mortal hazard to the Plantagenets, the previous royal family. The last female Plantagenet was Margaret Pole, Countess of Salisbury; although she was seventy years old and politically harmless, Henry VIII ordered her beheaded in 1541 on a spurious charge of treason. But proud Margaret refused to bow over the chopping block, telling her executioner that if he wanted her head, he could get it as best he might. She fled the axman, who chased her around Tower Green, gradually hacking her to death. Some claim that there is a ghostly reenactment of the grisly scene each May 27, its anniversary.

**Guilford Dudley.** Sickly and underage when he became king, Edward VI was a pawn for ambitious nobles. One of them was John Dudley, Duke of Northumberland, who married his son, Guilford Dudley, to Lady Jane Grey in hopes of winning the crown for his family. Lady Jane, grandniece of Henry VIII, had a tenuous claim to the throne. As King Edward was dying, Northumberland persuaded him to name Jane his successor, but soon after Edward's death, the populace recognized Henry's daughter Mary as the rightful heir. Queen for less than a fortnight, Jane was imprisoned in the Tower along with her husband, and soon thereafter both were beheaded. It is said that Dudley's ghost sometimes sits by a window in Beauchamp Tower, weeping, as Dudley himself did while waiting there for his execution.

**Anne Boleyn.** The second of Henry VIII's six wives, Anne Boleyn lost the king's favor when she failed to bear him a male heir—and when his wandering eye fell on Jane Seymour. Henry had Anne sentenced to death on dubious charges of adultery and treason. At Anne's request, a swordsman was imported from France for her execution: She feared mutilation under the clumsy ax, which often failed to sever a head with a single blow. The young queen died by the blade on Tower Green in 1536 and was buried in the Tower Chapel of Saint Peter ad Vincula. Her ghost, with head and without, has been reported in many parts of the Tower, including the chapel. There, a spectral Anne is said to lead a procession of ghostly lords and ladies who pace back and forth, then vanish.

**Sir Walter Raleigh.** Soldier, adventurer, scholar, and scientist, Sir Walter Raleigh was a favorite of Elizabeth I. Incurring her temporary displeasure, he earned himself a brief stay in the Tower in 1592, but his real problems began in 1603, when Elizabeth died and James I took the throne. The new king suspected Raleigh of plotting against him and had him convicted of treason, but Raleigh's public popularity led James to stay the execution. On the whole, the second imprisonment was not unpleasant. Raleigh's family was with him, and he was free to receive visitors, exercise, write, and pursue scientific experiments. He was released in 1616 to voyage to the New World in search of gold. But the expedition failed, and in its course Raleigh violated royal orders against molesting Spanish possessions. Spain demanded vengeance, and in 1618 James had Raleigh beheaded on the old treason charge. A battlement adjoining his apartments in the Bloody Tower came to be called Raleigh's Walk because he often strolled there. It is said that on moonlit nights his ghost walks the battlement still.

*Countess of Salisbury*

*Guilford Dudley*

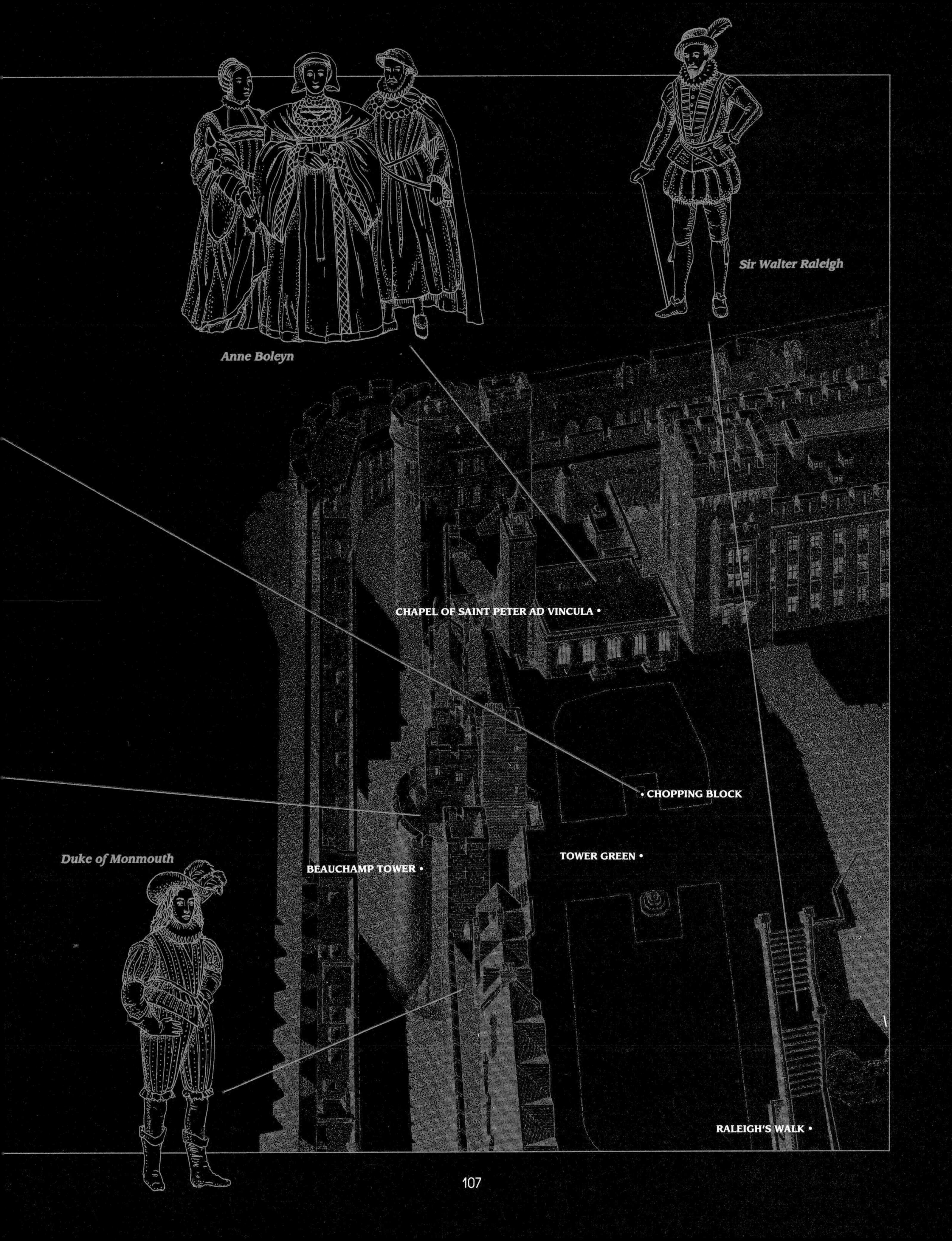
Anne Boleyn
Sir Walter Raleigh
CHAPEL OF SAINT PETER AD VINCULA •
• CHOPPING BLOCK
Duke of Monmouth
BEAUCHAMP TOWER •
TOWER GREEN •
RALEIGH'S WALK •

Phantom Bear
MARTIN TOWER
NORTHUMBERLAND'S WALK
Ghostly Vial
SALT TOWER

# A Spectral Bear and the Shade of Lady Jane Grey

**The Phantom Bear.** In the winter of 1815, a sentry was patrolling the entrance to the Martin Tower when, on the stroke of midnight, he saw a huge bear rear from beneath the door. The guard lunged with his bayonet, but the weapon passed through nothingness and lodged in the oak door. The terrified sentry fainted. The next day he was able to tell his story, but the day after that, he died—some said from fear. Though certainly a departure from ghostly lords and ladies, an apparitional bear in the Tower is not as misplaced as it seems. Henry I was the first king known to have kept a menagerie there, and the custom persisted through the centuries. Lions, tigers, zebras, monkeys, hyenas, and even elephants, as well as bears, were housed from time to time. The zoo was not eliminated until 1835, when a Tower lion mauled a soldier.

**The Earl of Northumberland.** In the year 1605, the wealthy and erudite Henry Percy, ninth earl of Northumberland, was sentenced to the Tower for complicity in the Gunpowder Plot, whose aim was to blow up Parliament—and along with it, King James I. He stayed there sixteen years before buying his freedom with a £30,000 fine. Like Sir Walter Raleigh, Northumberland had a relatively easy life in the Tower. His children were with him much of the time, and he was able to gather about him other learned inmates—Raleigh among them—for seminars on scientific and literary matters. The fact that the earl was treated well and allowed to leave the Tower with his head still affixed to his shoulders apparently did not, however, deter him from haunting the premises. His ghost is believed to walk the battlements abutting the Martin Tower, where, in life, the earl customarily took the air.

**The Ghostly Vial.** One of the strangest phantoms in all Tower lore appeared only once and has defied attempts to identify or explain it. One October evening in 1817, Edmund Lenthal Swifte, keeper of the crown jewels, was dining with his family in the Martin Tower, where the jewels were then kept. Suddenly, Swifte's wife shouted, "Good God! What is that?" Swifte looked up to see what appeared to be a glass cylinder, some three inches in diameter, filled with swirling white and pale blue liquids. The colors writhed and intermixed as the vial hovered above the table and then slowly moved behind Mrs. Swifte. She clutched at her shoulders and cried, "Oh, Christ! It has seized me." Swifte leaped to his feet and flung a chair at the tube, which disappeared instantly, never to be seen again.

**Lady Jane Grey.** In England, royal blood could be both rare honor and deadly taint. So it was for Lady Jane Grey, a victim of her father-in-law's abortive scheme to make her queen of England. Jane died under the Tower ax at the age of only fifteen. Prior to her own death, Jane had to watch from her prison window while her young husband was taken to his execution on Tower Hill. Later that same day, February 12, 1554, she was beheaded on Tower Green. Jane's ghost has been reported as recently as 1957, when, on the 403d anniversary of her death, a Tower guard spotted a white shape high on the battlemented roof of the Salt Tower. As he watched, the nebulous mass seemed to form itself into a likeness of Lady Jane. The guard called a second sentry, who also saw the queenly apparition.

*Earl of Northumberland*

*Lady Jane Grey*

# CHAPTER 4

# A World of Hauntings

ineteen-year-old Rosina Despard and her family had moved into their home—a handsome, three-story house on Pittville Circus Road in Cheltenham, England—only two months before she first encountered the woman in black. That moment occurred on a June evening in 1882. It was bedtime, and Rosina had just retired to her third-floor room when she heard a noise in the hall. Thinking it might be her mother, she opened the door. No one was there. She gingerly took a few steps down the dim hallway. The light from her candle flickered on the walls and ceiling. Suddenly, ahead of her at the top of the stairs, Rosina caught sight of a tall woman clad in a widow's mourning black, a veil concealing her face.

While the young woman watched, the figure descended the stairs in eerie stillness; when Rosina attempted to follow, her candle flame died, plunging her into pitch blackness. Rosina could hear nothing but the sound of her own breathing. She hurried back to her room and returned to bed. Thus began the haunting of the Despard household—a seven-year visitation that was reported by more than a dozen people and was set down, in copious and convincing detail, by the family member who had originally discovered the phantom widow.

No flighty adolescent, Rosina Despard was then a medical student, highly unusual for a woman in Victorian England or anywhere else at the time. By all accounts, she was a serious, level-headed person of scientific interests, not the type to spin fantasies. Yet she would report seeing the mysterious figure on many other occasions, in daylight and in darkness, often at the same stair landing outside her bedroom.

Several times, the student said, she followed it down to the drawing room on the first floor, where the ghostly figure would stand by the bay window for a few minutes before rustling into the hallway and disappearing toward a side door that opened onto a garden. The specter, which was usually seen with a handkerchief held to the face, never spoke, and it ignored Rosina whenever she addressed it. On several occasions Rosina tried to corner the figure, only to see it vanish. She tried to touch it—once even attempting to pounce on it—but the apparition always managed to elude her.

As an experiment she fastened threads just above the stairs, stretched taut from edge to edge, and watched as the figure passed right through them.

In the summer of 1884, two years after the initial sighting, the appearances became more frequent. One evening, Rosina and three of her four sisters reported they had seen the apparition, each independently of the other, as it stood in the drawing room and strolled in the garden and on the front lawn.

In certain respects, the behavior of the phantom widow conformed to the requirements of a classic haunted-house tale. Late at night came inexplicable "heavy thuds and bumpings," Rosina recalled. Other unsettling sounds were heard from time to time, the young woman noted—noises "of walking up and down on the second-floor landing, of bumps against the doors of the bedrooms, and of the handles of the doors turning." If such shenanigans did not intimidate Rosina, they certainly frightened the household staff. "Some left us on account of the noises," she wrote, "and we never could induce any of them to go out of their rooms after they had gone up for the night."

As a matter of fact, there seemed to be little cause for fear. For all her nocturnal meanderings, the spectral widow seemed oblivious to the mortals around her; her dolorous gaze carried no menace. And particularly in the earlier years of her sojourn, the apparition's appearance was so substantial and lifelike that she was often taken for an earthly visitor—a stranger in the house, but a human stranger—by those who glimpsed her. "At all times it intercepted the light," Rosina recalled. "We have not been able to ascertain if it cast a shadow."

Thanks to the tireless efforts of Frederic Myers, who learned of these bizarre events in late 1884, the Despard house remains perhaps the best-documented haunting case on record. Myers, the pioneer parapsychologist who two years before had helped found the London-based Society for Psychical Research, was thrilled by the opportunity to observe a haunting in progress, and he made the most of it, visiting the Cheltenham house several times to interview Rosina and her family. He would follow the case to the end, and it would strongly influence his seminal theories concerning the nature of apparitions. The researcher found a willing associate in Rosina and encouraged her on-site investigations—urging her, for example, to keep a camera ready to capture the ghost on film. (The bulky cameras and long photographic exposure times of the period made this impossible, however.)

Frederick Myers wrote a preface to Rosina Despard's account of the haunting, which appeared in the 1892 edition of the SPR *Proceedings* under the pseudonym of "Miss R. C. Morton." In her article, she concluded that the apparition was the ghost of a certain Imogen Swinhoe, the second wife of the man who originally owned the house. Rosina pointed out that the ghost's general appearance and habits coincided with those of Imogen, who had died in 1878, two years after her husband passed away and four years before the apparition first appeared to Rosina. Imogen Swinhoe was buried in a church cemetery just 500 yards from the house on Pittville Circus Road.

Fictional ghost stories, often with the apparition returning from the dead to torment some living person or to warn him or her of danger, have been a staple for writers since the beginnings of literature. But purported real-life ghost stories, such as the Cheltenham haunting, tend to be far more prosaic, frequently bearing little resemblance to their fictional counterparts.

The Despard story may well be the archetype of all incidents of haunting. These differ in fundamental ways from such related phenomena as the crisis apparition, in which a person suffering some trauma or other crisis reportedly appears to a loved one or friend, and the post-mortem apparition, in which the spirit of a long-deceased person is said to appear to one or several individuals in widely scattered places. A haunting is unrelated to any crisis and usually displays no purpose that would benefit either the apparition or the percipients. In addition, the ghost is often reported over a period of years by more than one person, but it does not show much awareness of the living people around it.

Finally and most importantly, a haunting is always linked to a specific place—a house, castle, stretch of road, or the like. Nor are haunted places restricted to the proverbial gloomy mansion set on a hill. At the White House in Washington, D.C., the ghost of Abraham Lincoln has reportedly been seen or sensed by Presidents Franklin D. Roosevelt and Dwight D. Eisenhower, and by Winston Churchill when he visited there.

Ghosts, it would seem, are creatures of habit. Often, as in the Cheltenham haunting, they appear to regularly reenact a kind of wistful ritual whose purpose can only be guessed at. The specter who haunted Rosina Despard's house typically was sighted at the drawing-room window, gazing at the garden and weeping silently. If, as Rosina believed, the apparition represented Imogen Swinhoe, only part of the mystery has been resolved. What cannot be answered is this: Why should Imogen, an alcoholic whose marriage, neighbors and friends agreed, was so unhappy that she left her husband some months before his death, return in the persona of a distraught widow?

The majority of alleged hauntings harbor such unknowable secrets at their core. In fact, one element that distinguishes hauntings from other kinds of phantom encounters is the ghost's inability or unwillingness to deliver a message to the living. Perhaps, the British psychical researcher Hilary Evans has written, "there are obstacles to such communication: But in that case, why does the entity persist in such futile efforts, often over what is to us a considerable time span? Is there nobody to tell the phantom it is wasting its time? Why are the spirits of the dead given the capability of making this kind of return visit, if they do so to so little effect?"

Of all the characteristics that define a ghost, visibility is not an essential one. The Cheltenham phantom was just as often heard as it was seen, and the files of haunted-house investigators are overflowing with reports of audible phantoms, tactile phantoms, and most elusive of all, phantoms that are perceived not through any of the physical

senses but through some alternate channel that defies explanation. The prominent British parapsychologist Andrew MacKenzie refers to such intangible encounters as "the sense of a presence."

Sometimes, it so happens, the presence is a venerable one. In 1867, while traveling through Switzerland, a married couple stopped at a château in the town of Nyon. Late that evening, with moonlight filling their bedchamber, the woman suddenly awakened "with a sort of certainty that a tall, thin old man in a long, flowered dressing gown was seated and writing at the table in the middle of the room. I cannot say what gave me this certainty, or this distinct picture, for I did not once turn my eyes to the place where I felt that the intruder was seated." In her state of panic, the woman awoke her husband, who gradually persuaded her to look at the writing table. To her complete surprise, she did not see anyone there.

The next morning at the landlord's apartment, when the woman's husband related the story, the nonchalant reply was: "Ah, you have seen Voltaire." It developed that in his later years, the great French philosopher had often visited the château, had stayed in the quarters now occupied by the couple—and, in that room, had been reportedly sensed and sometimes seen, long after his death in 1778, by generations of travelers.

No less a temple of traditional science than the Royal Institution of Great Britain in London is said to be the occasional dwelling of another renowned spirit. Over the years, a succession of scholars have somewhat sheepishly avowed that they have felt the nearness, in some form, of Michael Faraday, the nineteenth-century chemist and physicist who first demonstrated, among other things, the principle of the electromagnetic dynamo that underlies the modern electrical industry.

One witness, Dr. Eric Laithwaite, recounted how on two separate occasions in the 1960s he became aware that Faraday was at hand, guiding and assisting him in giving a lecture. "I'm not the only person to have spoken of this," said Laithwaite, a professor of engineering at London's Im-

***Since Abraham Lincoln's death in 1865, his ghost has allegedly haunted the White House—making its presence felt and seen most frequently, it is said, in Lincoln's former bedroom (far left). Some people even claim that a phantom of the funeral train that bore the slain President's body from Washington, D.C., to Springfield, Illinois, for burial, retraces the route every year on the anniversary of its passage.***

perial College. "You ask the others and you say: 'Where does he stand?' and they say: 'About there, you know, about there,' which is the same spot." And yet no one claims to have actually seen Faraday. His spirit, they say, is somehow just there.

Customarily, a haunting spirit announces its arrival in a more palpable fashion. With remarkable frequency, percipients report a sensation of cold accompanying a phantom encounter. The chill may originate inside the witnesses themselves, or it may be felt in the air surrounding them. The percipients may experience such a sensation even though they do not see or hear anything else mysterious. For example, an Englishwoman who took her two children to Blackpool for a week-long vacation was almost literally frozen with fear one night as the three slept in their boarding-house room.

"All at once I knew something had entered the room, and not through door or window," she reported. "I dared not open my eyes but just waited. Then the nape of my neck went icy cold, and up the back and over the top to my forehead as though a finger was drawn over, and my hair stood on end, I could actually feel my hair rising as the icy cold passed over my head, a short pause, and then it was repeated, another pause, repeated again, and then I knew it had gone and the room was clear." Unfortunately, it is unlikely that the woman troubled to inquire about the haunted history, if any, of her quarters. In her account, she simply stated that she had planned to take her children home the next day and was glad of it.

Vacationers or visitors or new residents of a town often provide some of the most persuasive testimony about hauntings, because such people probably would not know in advance the significance of what they witness. Such was the case with an Australian woman, Stella Herbert, who in 1965 went to stay with a friend, the owner of a small farm in the English village of Waresley. Mrs. Herbert retired early on her first night at Vicarage Farm and had long been asleep when, as she later reported, she was awakened by the figure of a little boy kneeling at her bedside. The child, who appeared emaciated, stared at Mrs. Herbert with a pleading gaze and proceeded to claw at her arm, which added considerably to her alarm.

Although the boy spoke not a word, Mrs. Herbert could sense he was imploring her to call his mother. Without intending to do so, she suddenly cried out, "Mummy," and with that the young visitor vanished.

Not surprisingly, this incident was much on her mind the next morning. After Mrs. Herbert related it all to her host, she was told that the boy was probably the ghost of Johnny Minney, the little brother of a tenant who still lived at Vicarage Farm. Johnny had died of meningitis more than forty years earlier. He had contracted the disease in 1921 in the very room where Mrs. Herbert slept. Johnny's sister, now a woman of middle age, remembered that their parents were away in London on the day he was stricken. Throughout that night, she said, he cried in pain and called constantly for "Mummy." Seven months later, at the age of four, he succumbed.

Assuming that the phantom in some way represented Johnny, a central question persists, one that also hovers over the Cheltenham haunting and so many others: What did Johnny want? And still more tantalizing: Why would he wait four decades and more to make such an important appearance? And why would he appear to Mrs. Herbert, a stranger? Neither Mrs. Herbert's friend nor the tenant, Johnny's sister, gave any hint that the ghost of Johnny Minney had ever come calling before.

To Mrs. Herbert, one of the most vivid aspects of Johnny's visit was the unmistakable sensation that the child was clutching at her. Instances in which a percipient is actually touched by a phantom are uncommon; even rarer are those cases in which a person can grasp a ghost, although there are reports of witnesses reaching out and shaking the hand of a spectral relative who is making a return visit. More often, though, when approached, the apparition fades away, disappears all at once, or allows the human hand to pass straight through it.

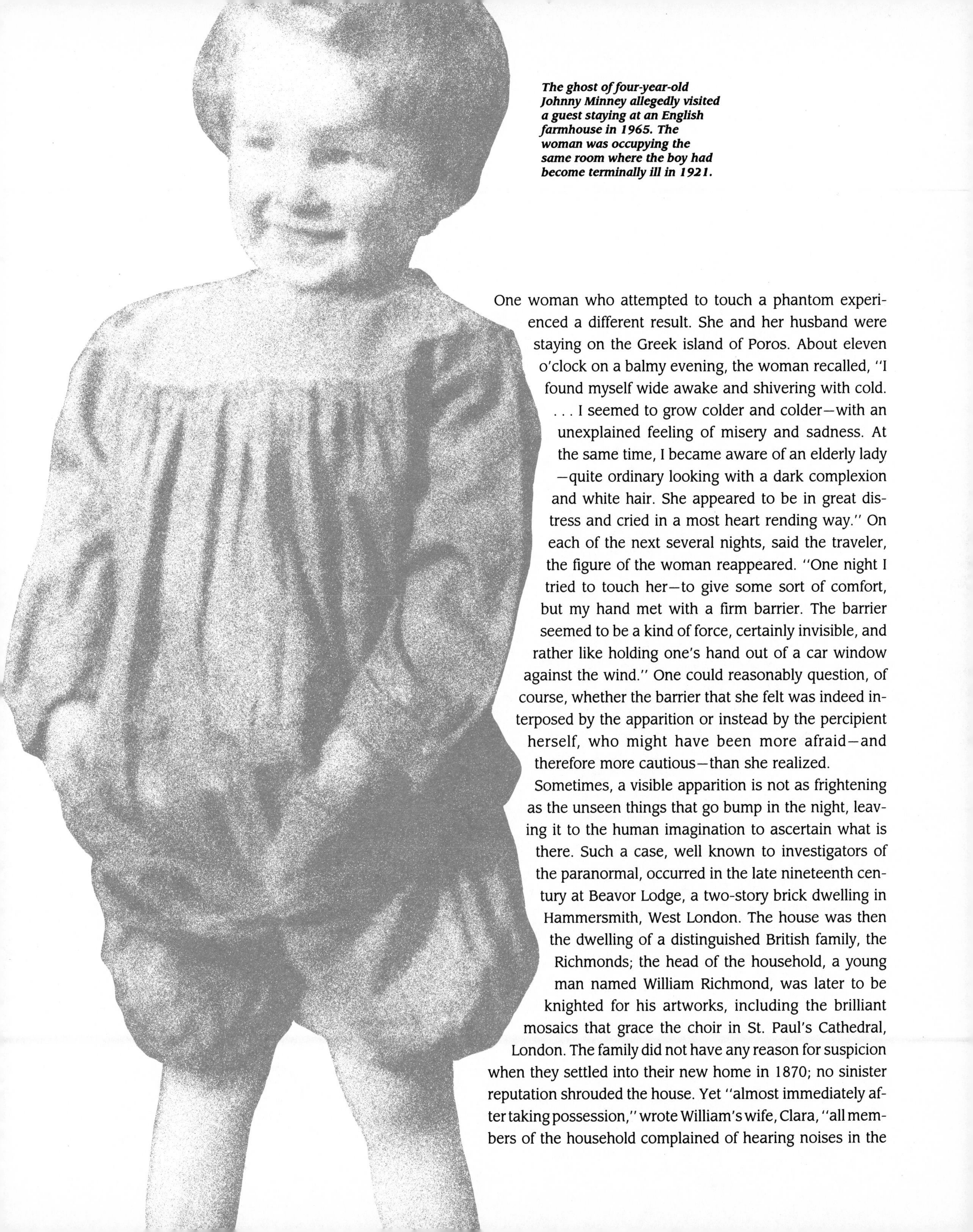

***The ghost of four-year-old Johnny Minney allegedly visited a guest staying at an English farmhouse in 1965. The woman was occupying the same room where the boy had become terminally ill in 1921.***

One woman who attempted to touch a phantom experienced a different result. She and her husband were staying on the Greek island of Poros. About eleven o'clock on a balmy evening, the woman recalled, "I found myself wide awake and shivering with cold. . . . I seemed to grow colder and colder—with an unexplained feeling of misery and sadness. At the same time, I became aware of an elderly lady—quite ordinary looking with a dark complexion and white hair. She appeared to be in great distress and cried in a most heart rending way." On each of the next several nights, said the traveler, the figure of the woman reappeared. "One night I tried to touch her—to give some sort of comfort, but my hand met with a firm barrier. The barrier seemed to be a kind of force, certainly invisible, and rather like holding one's hand out of a car window against the wind." One could reasonably question, of course, whether the barrier that she felt was indeed interposed by the apparition or instead by the percipient herself, who might have been more afraid—and therefore more cautious—than she realized.

Sometimes, a visible apparition is not as frightening as the unseen things that go bump in the night, leaving it to the human imagination to ascertain what is there. Such a case, well known to investigators of the paranormal, occurred in the late nineteenth century at Beavor Lodge, a two-story brick dwelling in Hammersmith, West London. The house was then the dwelling of a distinguished British family, the Richmonds; the head of the household, a young man named William Richmond, was later to be knighted for his artworks, including the brilliant mosaics that grace the choir in St. Paul's Cathedral, London. The family did not have any reason for suspicion when they settled into their new home in 1870; no sinister reputation shrouded the house. Yet "almost immediately after taking possession," wrote William's wife, Clara, "all members of the household complained of hearing noises in the

# The Quest for Ghostly Voices

The search for proof of the existence of ghosts has consumed the time and energy of any number of scientists, psychical investigators, and ghost hunters over the years. Most have toiled quietly and in obscurity. But when the phantom quest captured the attention of scientific genius Thomas A. Edison, whose achievements included the introduction of the electric light and invention of the phonograph, the entire world sat up and took notice.

Edison, it seems, had set to work on an apparatus that he hoped spirits would use to communicate with the living. Not that Edison admitted to believing in ghosts. It was his desire, he told a reporter in 1920, merely to construct a device that would give spirit beings, if they existed, "a better opportunity to express themselves than the tilting tables and raps and Ouija boards and mediums and the other crude methods now purported to be the only means of communication." In Edison's words, the device would be so sensitive "that the slightest effort which it intercepts will be magnified many times"—making it as valuable to the psychic researcher, he believed, as the microscope is to the scientist.

Whether the aging Edison had lapsed into senility, as many skeptics undoubtedly thought, or was poised to earn psychical research a place of respect in the scientific community, no one knows. His device for contacting ghosts remained shrouded in secrecy, either unsuccessful or incomplete at the time of his death in 1931. His theory, however, was taken up—and some would say proved—quite by accident in 1959 by a Russian-born painter, musician, and film producer named Friedrich Jürgenson.

***Shown here with his phonograph, the great inventor Thomas A. Edison hoped to devise an apparatus for communication with spirits.***

Jürgenson, who lived in a villa near Stockholm, had gone out to the countryside to capture the singing of finches with his battery-operated tape recorder. When he played the recording back, however, he heard—interspersed with the chirping of birds—what seemed to be human voices speaking in Swedish and Norwegian. Although the voices appeared to be discussing birds' songs, Jürgenson at first thought he had recorded a stray radio transmission. But subsequent tapings contained sounds that he interpreted as messages from his deceased friends and relatives. These purported communications were spoken quickly, he said, and with a peculiar cadence that was alien to the ear.

Jürgenson repeated his experiments over the next few years, recording spectral sounds both indoors and out. In 1964, he published his findings in a book titled *Voices from the Universe.* Among the scientists who were intrigued by his story was Konstantin Raudive, a Latvian-born parapsychologist and former psychology professor living in Sweden. Raudive asked Jürgenson to play some tapes for him and a few colleagues. Jürgenson cheerfully agreed, and also recorded a

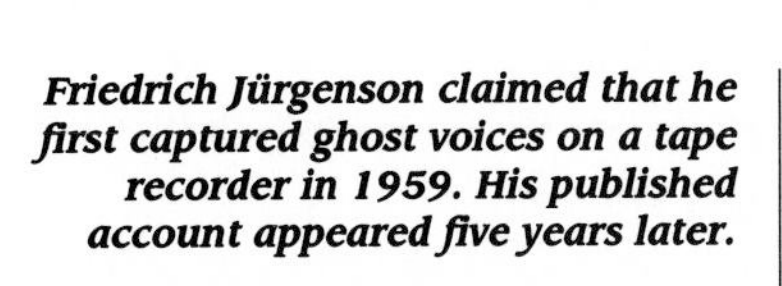

*Friedrich Jürgenson claimed that he first captured ghost voices on a tape recorder in 1959. His published account appeared five years later.*

*Impressed by Friedrich Jürgenson's electronic voice discovery, parapsychologist Konstantin Raudive devoted nine years to recording and analyzing the sounds on tens of thousands of tapes.*

tape in their presence, interpreting the voices for the admiring group.

Raudive immediately embraced Jürgenson's discovery, viewing it as an opportunity to prove, through empirical scientific methods, that some form of life existed after physical death. The two men collaborated in researching the so-called electronic voices until 1969, when differences led them to part company.

Raudive continued to investigate the phenomenon, using an ordinary reel-to-reel tape recorder to make more than 100,000 recordings. At times he attached his equipment to a radio, believing that voices could be detected in the white noise found between frequencies. Raudive claimed to recognize many of the voices he heard on the tapes, and some of them allegedly identified themselves. Among his reported contacts were Adolf Hitler, Carl Jung, and Johann Wolfgang von Goethe.

An exhaustive account of Raudive's work, which included a small phonograph record containing samples of the alleged voices, was published in 1968. A short time later, Raudive claimed he was visited by engineers from the National Aeronautics and Space Administration (NASA). The American visitors refused to explain their interest in his project, Raudive reported, but examined his experiments and asked "unusually pertinent questions."

The book also aroused the interest of a number of skeptics in what came to be known as the "Raudive voices." Some dismissed the voices as an imaginative interpretation of radio static or the tape recorder's hum, while others believed that Raudive had mistaken fragments of foreign-language radio broadcasts for the murmurings of spirits.

Undaunted, Raudive continued his research until his death in September 1974. At a conference on the paranormal ten days later in Germany, a recorder was set up in case Raudive's ghost decided to provide the proof of a spirit existence that had eluded the scientist in life. Although some claimed to detect Raudive's voice on the tape, no coherent revelation from the spirit world was forthcoming. The intriguing legacy of Raudive, Jürgenson, and Edison is now in the hands of modern researchers, who continue to seek, through electronic means, communication with the dead.

lower part of the house—windows would be violently shaken every night between two and four o'clock, and steps were heard apparently going about the house. I myself frequently had doors opened for me before entering a room, as if a hand had hastily turned the handle and thrown it open. Then occasionally we used to hear sounds as of someone sobbing and sighing."

There seemed to be voices too. Mrs. Richmond, under the impression that her husband was summoning her, would go to him and discover he had not spoken. Mr. Richmond, likewise, would hear a voice beckoning, "Willie! Willie!" He would rush to his wife, only to learn that she had not called for him.

To the family's growing alarm, the peculiar stirrings continued for five years. And then one afternoon, as Clara Richmond sat reading to three of her children, the dining-room door opened and in strode a short woman dressed in gray muslin. Mrs. Richmond had never seen her before. After a long, bewildering moment, the woman turned to leave. But before she could reach the door, Mrs. Richmond wrote, "she seemed to dissolve away."

The female figure revisited Beavor Lodge from time to time. She was reportedly seen by servants, by William Richmond, by the Richmonds' six-year-old daughter, and by a few others. But what left the deepest impression on the household were the inexplicable noises. (Later, an investigator from the SPR would conclude that the most likely source of these sounds was an underground waterway beneath the house.)

One Richmond family friend was awakened in her guest room at midnight by what appeared to be the thunderous sound of carriages on the lane just outside the window of her room. Such an unusual clatter that late at night left her too curious and frightened to sleep. During the next three hours, the woman—who dared not move from her bed—thought she heard from the room below animated

***When the British World War II bomber called S for Sugar was moved to a London museum, the ghosts of its crew were rumored to have gone along. On occasion, phantom gunners dressed in full flying gear reportedly have been seen manning the plane's turrets.***

talking and hearty laughter, a fusillade of footsteps, as well as doors opening and closing: a festive phantom party. Early the next morning, the woman mustered the courage to inspect the room below; she found it completely undisturbed, every piece of furniture in its place.

In the preponderance of reputed hauntings, the phantom and its mission are apparently unknown to the percipient. That characteristic, which helps distinguish hauntings from post-mortem or crisis apparitions, does not always hold true, however. The lines separating the various categories of phantom encounters can be as blurry as the apparitions themselves. Witness the ghost of Grandfather Bull, which allegedly haunted a country cottage in Wiltshire, England, during the winter of 1932.

Samuel Bull, a former chimney sweep, had died the previous year of cancer, a disease common to those in his occupation. The man had left behind an aged widow, their daughter, and six grandchildren, all of whom were crowded into a house so dilapidated that parts of it had been officially declared unfit for habitation. The daughter, a Mrs. Edwards, occupied a downstairs bedroom along with three of her children. One frigid February night, they were alarmed to see Grandfather Bull go by their doorway, up the stairs, and through a closed door into the very room where he had died and where his widow now lay sleeping. Apparently, he approached her side and gently placed a cool, comforting hand on her brow.

The apparition visited regularly over the next several months, appearing at all hours of the day and night to startled members of the family, who at first were frightened but gradually grew to accept it. Before each encounter, a vague feeling of restless expectation—the sense of a presence—reportedly stole over everyone in the household. At all times, the ghost looked solid, three-dimensional. It spoke only once, when it addressed the widow Bull by her given name, Jane. On at least one occasion, it was visible for several hours—in the annals of documented hauntings, an unusually long time.

As much as anything else, the family became aware of the sorrowful expression worn by Grandfather Bull and attributed it to the squalid conditions in which they were forced to live. Not long after the ghost's first manifestation, however, the family received welcome news: A vacancy was imminent in far more pleasant public housing. At this possible improvement in their situation, Mrs. Edwards remarked, the ghost's appearance grew cheerier. It even seemed to glow, so that at night it could be seen without benefit of candlelight. When the family received confirmation of the move to public housing, the visitations stopped altogether.

A more durable spirit is said to be in residence at the Theatre Royal on Drury Lane, London. Indeed, if the legends are to be believed, that house shelters a veritable ensemble cast of the nether world. A gaunt, hatchet-faced figure often seen slouching across the orchestra pit is reputedly a mercurial Irish actor who murdered a colleague in 1735. The ghost of the nineteenth-century Shakespearean player Charles Kean has also been sighted, and the spectral visage of a deceased comedian named Dan Leno once seemed to materialize in the dressing-room mirror of a pantomime artist who was preparing to go on stage.

But the most venerable ghost of Drury Lane is known simply as "the man in gray." The figure, a handsome, courtly young man attired in an eighteenth-century riding cloak and boots, wearing a tricorne hat and brandishing a sword, has allegedly stalked the aisles of that famous auditorium for generations.

Walter James MacQueen-Pope, a historian of the London theatrical world, reported the unnerving experience of a cleaning woman who began her work in the not-quite-deserted upper circle one morning in 1938. "She saw, sitting in the end seat on the center gangway of the fourth row, a figure of a man in gray, wearing a hat, gazing down at the stage. She thought it one of the actors, who had assumed his costume, but also thought she had better make sure. She therefore put down her pail and her broom and went to speak to the figure. As she neared it, it seemed to

EXIT

***One alleged patron of London's Theatre Royal holds no ticket—he is a phantom known as the "man in gray." The figure, dressed in eighteenth-century costume, is thought to be the ghost of a man whose skeleton was found—still with a dagger in his side—enclosed in a small space in the theater's upper circle. The specter reportedly walks across the circle, and then disappears into a wall near where the gruesome discovery was made.***

vanish, and then reappeared at the exit door . . . . She had never heard of the ghost before in her life, but gave a description of it which tallied accurately with all the others."

The man in gray is surely among the most benign ghosts known. Actors, by nature a superstitious lot, swear the apparition brings good luck. They cite the ghost's appearance before the opening nights at Drury Lane of *Oklahoma!, Carousel, The King and I,* and *South Pacific* as a harbinger of the long runs enjoyed by those Rodgers and Hammerstein musicals.

It stands to reason that a ghost would be at home in the theater. Phantoms are rather convincing actors, after all, playing as they so often do the role of living human beings—moving, dressing, in some cases even speaking in a most lifelike way. But an apparition need not assume human form. For instance, a woman who lived for a time in a ground-floor apartment in Sydney, Australia, told researchers she was visited each night by an invisible cat. "It was so vivid," the woman recalled. "I could feel it jumping onto the bed from the windowsill, and it would then walk up me toward my face. It seemed so real that I often involuntarily (while still reading, I became so used to it) put up my hand to stop it from walking on my face . . . . Eventually we became so used to one another that I heard the little creature purr, though I never saw it."

Reports of apparitional cats—some visible—are not uncommon. Still more widespread and time-honored are tales of the "black dog," a ghostly creature sighted for centuries in continental Europe, Canada, parts of the United States—and particularly in the British Isles.

Typically, the beast takes the form of a large, coal-black dog, shoulder high or even bigger, with fiery eyes; it is seen to patrol—virtually to haunt—a length of country lane and then vanish. Nearly every shire throughout England can boast its own lurid variation on the theme. In one such legend, a wagon driver strikes at the dog and is instantly incinerated. In another, a farmer confronting the animal is rendered paralyzed and speechless.

# The Spirits of Versailles

Paris had been sweltering during the summer of 1901, but on August 10 the heat was mitigated by light clouds and a lively wind. For Annie Moberly *(above)* and Eleanor Jourdain *(right),* two English academics on vacation, it was a perfect day for a stroll through the nearby city of Versailles.

After touring the exquisite Palace of Versailles, the women decided to visit the Petit Trianon *(top),* a residence built in 1762 for the mistress of Louis XV and later frequented by Marie Antoinette. As they walked through the gardens, Miss Jourdain reported later, she experienced "a feeling of depression and loneliness." When the ladies arrived at a garden kiosk, her disquiet escalated into an "impression of something uncanny and fear inspiring."

The women hurried toward the Petit Trianon, encountering several people along the path, including two men in "greyish-green coats with small three-cornered hats" standing near a cottage, a man in a slouched hat and black cloak, and a woman sitting on the ground, sketching.

While the visit itself was uneventful, both women felt that something odd had happened to them in Versailles, and they concluded that the place was haunted. On return trips, they found that the kiosk and the oddly dressed men had disappeared, the cottage looked quite different, and a well-rooted shrub grew on the spot where the artist had been seated. The women studied the Petit Trianon's history and concluded that they had somehow witnessed a scene from the period of Marie Antoinette. In 1911 they recounted their story in a book titled *An Adventure.*

That same year Eleanor Sidgwick of the Society for Psychical Research reviewed the women's case and found it muddled. But reports of ghostly figures in the Versailles gardens continued to accumulate, capturing the attention in 1946 of psychical researcher G. W. Lambert. Lambert concluded that some details reported by Moberly and Jourdain, and corroborated by others, were inconsistent with the Versailles scenery in 1901 but similar to historical descriptions of the location in 1770.

He felt that the two women may have experienced retrocognition, in which a person living in the present allegedly observes past events. Skeptics, however, have speculated that the women actually saw actors in costume rehearsing a play. Whatever they witnessed, it is likely that the skeptics and those who believe ghosts inhabit Versailles will continue to debate this intriguing case for years to come.

In 1972 in rural Dartmoor, according to one account, a couple were awakened by the sound of scratching outside their door. The man grabbed a poker, went to investigate—and found himself face to face with an immense black dog, its eyes glowing like red-hot coals. As he swung at it, the dog vanished in an explosion of light and the sound of shattering glass. A tour of the house revealed that every window was broken, the electricity had failed, and the yard was littered with roof shingles; it was as if the house had been struck by a tornado.

The two most notorious incidents reportedly took place on the same stormy Sunday in the county of Suffolk in 1577. Churches in Bungay and Blythburgh, two villages seven miles apart, were wracked by the specter of a black dog that appeared among the parishioners just as a fierce thunderstorm was breaking. In Bungay, according to a chronicler of the era, Abraham Fleming, the dog passed between two members of the congregation, and "as they were kneeling uppon their knees, and occupied in prayer as it seemed, wrung the necks of them bothe at one instant clene backward, insomuch that even at a moment where they kneeled, they strangely dyed."

Fleming, in a volume titled *A Straunge and Terrible Wunder,* went on to give a picturesque account of the carnage at the second church, at Blythburgh: "On the selfsame day, in like manner, into the parish church of another towne called Blibery, not above seven miles distant from Bongay above said, the like thing Entred, in the same shape and similitude, where placing himself uppon a maine balke or beam, whereon some ye Rood did stand, sodainely he gave a swinge downe through ye church, and there also, as before, slew two men and a lad, and burned the hand of another person that was there among the rest of the company, of whom diverse were blasted.

"This mischief thus wrought, he flew with wonderful force to no little feare of the assembly, out of the church in a hideous and hellish likeness."

In defense of the black dog, it should be noted that inhabitants of many localities in Britain consider it a friendly phantom. It is sometimes regarded as the guardian of women and children who travel solitary rural roads. Elsewhere, the dog's appearance is often interpreted as merely an omen of bad weather, a belief that may derive from the ferocious storm on that long-ago Sunday morning in Bungay and Blythburgh.

Some psychical researchers who have studied the enduring legend of the black dog offer an intriguing theory to explain the phenomenon. They believe that many ancient sites in Britain, such as hill forts, burial mounds, and stone circles, were laid out according to a pattern of terrestrial force lines. Many of these so-called ley lines, the investigators believe, were held to be sacred and at one time were guarded by dogs. It is conceivable, proponents of the theory say, that ancient monuments might act as "recording devices" for images of events long past, and that a resonance created by the ley lines could make these images visible to psychically sensitive people. If this is correct, the black dogs haunting the English countryside could be the spectral images of ancient guard dogs.

Whether ghosts present themselves as snarling dogs or restless people, verifying their existence in a traditional scientific manner has proved impossible. A significant problem confronting any would-be ghost hunter is timing. A haunting can be reported over years, even decades or centuries, and a phantom's appearances generally are intermittent—it may show itself numerous times over a period of weeks, then go into hiding indefinitely.

Most ghosts appear to take a dark delight in foiling even the cleverest efforts of investigators, showing themselves when and to whom they choose but almost never when someone desires to see them. Rosina Despard discovered this tendency in her dogged campaign to document the visits of the Cheltenham ghost. "The figure was not called up by a desire to see it," the woman wrote, "for on every occasion when we made special arrangements to watch for it, we never saw it."

The frustrating elusiveness of ghosts has done little to

# Phantoms on Film

At an ancient castle in northern Italy, near Turin, midnight may truly be the witching hour. For it is said that in the morning's first hours, the ghosts of the Castello de la Rotta appear.

As many as seventeen vaporous figures reportedly haunt the castle. Some of the alleged ghosts are assumed to be Knights Templars, members of an influential and wealthy religious order that occupied the estate for more than two centuries. Fear of their power and a desire for their riches led King Philip IV of France to accuse the Templars of heresy and to suppress the order in 1312. Many knights were tortured to death and others burned at the stake.

Other castle spirits are thought to be victims of a plague that struck in 1631, when over 300 diseased bodies were buried under the castle's portico. And during the 1639 French invasion of Turin, thousands of people were killed and many bodies thrown into the castle's well.

In recent years, the castle and its supposed ghosts have become something of a tourist attraction, thanks in part to Count Augusto Olivero. An established Turin lawyer who lives with his family in a restored wing of the castle, Olivero seems unruffled by his spectral housemates. In fact, he regularly invites serious observers to come with their cameras for a midnight ghost-watching vigil.

Olivero personally guides his visitors into the castle's interior courtyard, where one specter, photographed by Olivero in 1982 *(right, top),* was allegedly seen walking under the portico toward the chapel. Another figure, thought to be a Knight Templar, emerged from a brick wall near the chapel *(right, center)* in 1984, during filming by a local television station. And in the empty chapel itself, in 1987, a woman reported seeing a slim column of bluish light, about four feet high. The light, which some interpret as the figure of a monk, allegedly wore a shroudlike garment and answered questions put forth by Olivero by glowing once for yes and twice for no.

A less expressive shade supposedly haunts the tower of Castello de la Rotta. Legend has it that a young woman, forced to marry the castle's elderly owner, threw herself from the tower on her wedding night. At times a woman's apparition has been reported near the tower, followed by the chilling sound of a scream. And every year, on June 15, it is said, a procession of ghosts assembles in the courtyard to mark the anniversary of her death. One year, Olivero captured two alleged participants on film *(below).*

But the ghost who is said to appear most often is called Arturo. Witnesses claim this hooded, skeletal figure wears a cross around his neck and gallops through the castle corridors on a skeletal horse. In 1980, two days after Count Olivero's discovery of the remains of a horse, a rider, and an iron cross buried in the dry, overgrown moat, Arturo supposedly materialized for a group of observers and was photographed *(right, bottom).*

Skeptics offer a number of earthly explanations for the appearances of Arturo and the other resident spirits. But those who believe in phantoms continue to regard the Castello de la Rotta as home for many ghosts of Italy's past.

ghost? An ESP projection? Imagination? No one could be completely sure.

American parapsychologist Michaeleen Maher, a student of Schmeidler's, employs similar techniques in her investigations of paranormal experiences. First she interviews percipients to determine their credibility. The degree of consistency among accounts and the circumstances surrounding the percipients' experiences both figure in her decision of whether to proceed further.

Next, she writes a detailed who-what-when description of all observed phenomena. Like Schmeidler, she inscribes data on a floor plan of the allegedly haunted site, then brings in psychics to walk through the house one by one with blank sets of plans, noting anything unusual. To provide a point of comparison, Maher repeats the procedure with two other groups, one of which is composed of people who make no claims of possessing psychic powers and the other made up of people who have a skeptical attitude toward the paranormal.

Maher's routine is based on her conviction that paranormal activity can be sensed only by people who are sympathetic or at least neutral toward the possibility that it exists. If the psychics and family members agree but skeptics disagree, Maher's view is that something paranormal—whether ESP or the actual presence of a ghost—is occurring. If all of the groups agree, however, what they are sensing is probably some natural stimulus (wind, animal noises, sounds produced by underground water) that is being misinterpreted as paranormal.

The late British archaeologist and historian Thomas C. Lethbridge proposed that paranormal activity might be explained by human "psyche fields" existing outside normal time and space. An enthusiastic dowser, he believed that water was an especially sensitive medium for the recording of these fields. By extension, he suggested, a ghost might be explained as a kind of psychic hologram, an image produced in a place by some strong thought or emotion years before and picked up later by people attuned to it.

The idea that such psychic energy can exist received a boost in the 1960s as a result of a series of experiments conducted by Graham Watkins, an associate with the Foundation for Research on the Nature of Man, founded in 1962 by the pioneering parapsychologist J. B. Rhine and his wife, Louisa. Watkins anesthetized pairs of mice, then tested the ability of alleged psychics to awaken one of the mice through extrasensory perception. He reported that at least a few of his subjects were able to accomplish this feat a statistically significant number of times.

An even more intriguing discovery was something that the researcher dubbed the linger effect. In this experiment, the pairs of mice were always placed in the same position. Subjects who were asked to communicate exclusively with either the left or right mouse always performed much better than they did when they divided their attention between one mouse and the other. Graham Watkins suggested that the subject was building up a "psychic vortex," or a force field fixed in space. Some researchers believe that such a field could explain hauntings: A psychic vortex created by the agent of the haunting might be able to linger in a house even if the tenant had left the place long ago—or had passed away.

Watkins also monitored his subjects' heartbeats and other physiological signals and found that the people performed better during certain states of mental and bodily activity. Enhancing these signals through biofeedback—the self-control of supposedly involuntary functions such as heartbeat—further improved results.

Like so many laboratory experiments in the field of psychical studies, Watkins's work with psychics and sedated mice has yet to be reproduced by other investigators. But if his findings are ever buttressed through further research, many will find it hard to resist the conclusion, in the words of the writer D. Scott Rogo, that hauntings, "which are often linked to tragedy, death or great emotional upheaval, are produced by an agent who has accidentally slipped into that psychophysiological state which can set up the force field. This field, in turn, generates a haunting."

# The Specters of War

If violent death can cause a spirit to linger at the scene of its earthly demise, then battlefields should be among the most haunted of the world's places. And indeed, ghostly armies and spectral soldiers have been reported many times and in many nations.

Ancient Greek scribes wrote of the fearsome plains of Marathon, north of Athens, where Athenian infantrymen repelled the Persians in 490 B.C. For years afterward, visitors to the battlefield talked of hearing the whistle of spears and the screams of dying men; some even claimed to see the combatants themselves, bronze-clad Athenians struggling with Persians behind wicker shields. British history abounds with similar stories—evidence either of the psychic nature of the misty isles or to the English love of a good ghost story. The civil war of 1642-48 alone yielded three phantom battle scenes—the engagements at Naseby, Marston Moor, and Edgehill *(page 134)*—two of them allegedly reenacted in the sky. In the modern era, two world wars have supposedly left ghostly traces in sites from Dieppe to Burma.

Believers who seek the reasons for these scenes have several theories. Some feel that the enormous amount of terror and pain experienced on the battlefield leaves a psychic residue. Others guess at retrocognition, or timeslips, rare moments when past and present collide. Whatever the explanation, the stories are vivid testimonies to the lingering horrors of war. Five such tales are illustrated on the following ten pages.

# Ghostly Warriors from the Heart of Cadbury Hill

The gentle West Country of England is a land of legend. Fairies and phantoms are said to walk its hills; supernatural hounds reportedly prowl the bogs of Dartmoor. But perhaps the most potent of West Country tales comes from Cadbury Castle in the county of Somerset. The ramparts of this overgrown Iron Age fort encircle a hill that is reputed to be not only hollow but inhabited.

An anonymous schoolteacher added to the area's reputation for the eerie when she told of a strange procession she witnessed on Cadbury Hill in the 1930s. As she and a companion drove past it late one night, she said, they saw a collection of bright lights parading slowly down the hill. Closer inspection revealed the lights to be torches, strapped to the lances of a troop of armed warriors. A huge mounted man led the soldiers into the darkness, and all vanished.

The schoolteacher's tale might be just another ghost story were it not for Cadbury's legendary occupants. According to local tradition, the hill was once the site of King Arthur's court. Archaeologists confirm that the ancient fort could have housed a chieftain in the sixth century, when the warrior known as Arthur fought the Saxons. For centuries, villagers have claimed that Arthur slumbers with his soldiers within Cadbury Hill and rides forth by moonlight on patrol. He waits, they say, for an embattled England to call him to service once more.

# A Torchlight Search for the Dead of Nechtansmere

The Scottish night was ank, with rain changing to snow, and the oads were treacherous as Miss E. F. Smith lrove home from a party on January 2, 1950. ight miles from her house in the isolated illage of Letham, the car skidded off the oad and into a ditch, leaving Miss Smith vith no choice but to walk with her small log the rest of the way.

It was about 2:00 A.M. when the woman pproached Letham, by this time carrying ier pet on her shoulder. As she crested a iill, she saw what she later called "an in-redible thing." In a distant field, moving igures carrying crimson torches walked a ircuitous path, seeming to skirt the edge of ome invisible barrier. As Miss Smith drew loser to the scene, she saw that the figures vere men dressed in tights and short tunics, vho seemed to be searching the ground—erhaps for bodies, she thought. At this oint, her dog began to growl, and Miss mith hurried home, concerned that the an-mal would wake the villagers.

The woman's story, repeated to friends, ventually reached the Society for Psychical Research, whose investigators concluded hat Miss Smith might well have seen a hostly reenactment of the Battle of Nech-ansmere. Fought along the shores of a shal-ow lake in A.D. 685, the brutal clash of Picts nd Northumbrians ended with the death of cgfrith, King of Northumbria, and a com-lete Pictish victory. Perhaps, speculated the esearchers, the spectral scene represented he Picts retrieving their dead from the anks of the long-vanished loch.

# Aerial Echoes of the Battle of Edgehill

The first pitched battle
of the English civil war took place on October 23, 1642, when the forces of King
Charles I fought those of Parliamentarian
Robert Devereux, third Earl of Essex, around
a high, scrubby ridge called Edgehill, about
thirty miles north of Oxford. It was not a de-
cisive engagement. Throughout the long,
weary day, cavalrymen wielding swords
and pistols charged and retreated in a dis-
orderly swirl. The next morning, unable to
claim victory, both armies marched away to
lick their wounds.

About two months later, travelers passing
Edgehill late at night were alarmed to hear
the roll of distant drums. As described in a
1643 pamphlet entitled in part "A Great
Wonder in Heaven," the witnesses saw "in
the air the same incorporeal soldiers that
made these clamours, . . . one army . . . having the King's colours, and the other the
Parliament's at their head. . . . Till two or
three in the morning . . . continued this
dreadful fight, the clattering of arms, noises
of cannon, cries of soldiers . . . amazing and
terrifying the poor men." The travelers reported the aerial battle to local authorities,
who returned with them the next night and
saw the same scene reenacted. Royalist officers ordered to Edgehill by King Charles to
quell the bizarre rumors also saw the ghostly armies and "recognised on the Royalist
side several of their personal friends who
had been killed." All of the witnesses swore
to the reality of their vision.

# The Phantom Soldier of Gallipoli

The hills of Turkey's Gallipoli Peninsula were still pocked by World War I foxholes when Leon Weeks arrived in the early 1950s. The American archaeologist set up camp in a lonely area, hoping to find relics from the disastrous Allied campaign of 1915-16. He may have found more than he bargained for.

One evening as he stood outside his tent smoking a cigarette, he saw a man scrambling down a nearby hill. The shadowy figure led a donkey, whose awkward burden looked much like a human body. Weeks pursued the strange pair, calling after them, but they disappeared before he could reach them. The next night the archaeologist saw them again, more clearly this time, and could even distinguish the gleam of leather boots on the donkey's cargo. Night after night the two appeared, but Weeks could never catch up with them. He had to leave the area without solving the mystery.

In 1968, while visiting a British friend, Weeks was examining the man's extensive stamp collection. There, among the Australian commemoratives, was a stylized version of the scene Weeks remembered witnessing so many years before: a man leading a donkey that bore a wounded soldier. The stamp, his friend explained, was issued in 1965 to honor the heroism of Private John Simpson Kirkpatrick, an English-born soldier who served as a stretcher bearer during the Gallipoli campaign. Kirkpatrick and his donkey had been a familiar sight on the battlefield, saving the lives of hundreds of wounded soldiers before the man was killed by shrapnel in May of 1915. He was buried amid the rocks of Gallipoli.

# The Restless Gunners of Hollandia

In the South Pacific, the battles of World War II often took on a grim and murky aspect. And for some, it seemed, those nightmarish experiences had no end. For instance, in the late 1950s, a reporter for the British Broadcasting Corporation described the apparent haunting of a house in Kuala Selangor, Malaysia. Once occupied by Japanese officers, the house was said to echo still with the sounds of a heavy-booted intruder. Other sources reported that fishermen on Corregidor, the hotly contested Philippine island, had seen spectral patrols for years after the war. Even Reuters, the respected British news service, took notice of a tale coming out of the northern coast of New Guinea.

The island's port of Hollandia had been the scene of a major Allied invasion in the spring of 1944. To secure this jumping-off point for the Philippines, forces under General Douglas MacArthur launched an attack on the harbor. Surprised and outgunned, the Japanese troops fled eastward, and the Allies moved in.

Local inhabitants would claim later that some of the Japanese remained behind, at least in spirit. In 1956, Reuters reported that natives of Hollandia had petitioned members of a visiting Japanese War Graves Commission to exorcise a decrepit antiaircraft gun abandoned on the beach. Every night at midnight, they claimed, haggard Japanese phantoms in rusty helmets rose to man the gun. Perhaps, they suggested, Buddhist priests could appease the angry spirits. It is not recorded, however, whether such a ceremony was ever performed, or if the troubled ghosts ever found their rest.

## ACKNOWLEDGMENTS

The index for *Phantom Encounters* was prepared by Hazel Blumberg-McKee. The editors wish to thank the following individuals and institutions for their valuable assistance in the preparation of this volume:
Prof. Hans Bender, Institut für Grenzgebiete der Psychologie und Psychohygiene, Freiburg, West Germany; Theo Brown, Exeter, England; Jean-Loup Charmet, Paris; Nick Clarke-Lowes, Society for Psychical Research, London; Hilary Evans, London; Maria and Alberto Fenoglio, Turin, Italy; Fondation Alexandra David-Neel, Digne-les-Bains, France; Leif Geiges, Staufen, West Germany; Paola Giovetti, Modena, Italy; Conte Augusto Olivero Grimaldi, Moncalieri, Turin, Italy; Captain Winfried Heinemann, Militärgeschichtliches, Freiburg, West Germany; Else Lugli, Turin, Italy; Andrew MacKenzie, London; Eleanor O'Keefte, Society for Psychical Research, London; Gian Marco Rinaldi, Torre del Lago, Lucca, Italy; William Roll, Psychical Research Foundation, Carrolltop, Georgia; Dr. Rolf Streichardt, Institut für Grenzgebiete der Psychologie und Psychohygiene, Freiburg, West Germany; Alan Wesencraft, Harry Price Library, London.

## BIBLIOGRAPHY

Abbott, G., *Ghosts of the Tower of London.* North Pomfret, Vt.: David & Charles, 1986.
Addiss, Stephen, ed., *Japanese Ghosts & Demons: Art of the Supernatural.* New York: George Braziller, 1985.
Alcock, Leslie, *Was This Camelot? Excavations at Cadbury Castle 1966-1970.* New York: Stein and Day, 1972.
Alexander, John, *Ghosts: Washington's Most Famous Ghost Stories.* Washington, D.C.: Washingtonian Books, 1975.
Alexander, Marc:
*Haunted Castles.* London: Frederick Muller, 1974.
*Haunted Churches and Abbeys of Britain.* London: Arthur Barker, 1978.
*Phantom Britain.* London: Frederick Muller, 1975.
Anderson, Jean, *The Haunting of America.* Boston: Houghton Mifflin, 1973.
Auerbach, Loyd, *ESP, Hauntings and Poltergeists: A Parapsychologist's Handbook.* New York: Warner Books, 1986.
Baird, A. T., *One Hundred Cases for Survival after Death.* London: T. Werner Laurie, 1944.
Bardens, Dennis, *Ghosts and Hauntings.* New York: Taplinger, 1968.
Borg, Alan, consult. ed., *Strange Stories from the Tower of London.* Harrisburg, Pa.: Historical Times, 1983.
Brown, Raymond Lamont:
*A Casebook of Military Mystery.* Cambridge: Patrick Stephens, 1974.
*Phantom Soldiers.* New York: Drake, 1975.
Cavendish, Richard, *Man, Myth & Magic.* New York: Marshall Cavendish, 1985.
Chambers, Aidan, *Book of Ghosts and Hauntings.* Harmondsworth, England: Longman Young Books, 1973
Charley, T., *News from the Invisible World: A Collection of Remarkable Narratives on the Certainty of Supernatural Visitations from the Dead to the Living.* London: S. D. Ewins.
Christie-Murray, David, "Stalked by a Nightmare." *The Unexplained* (London), Vol. 10, Issue 110.
Clarke, Ida Clyde, *Men That Wouldn't Stay Dead: Twenty-Six Authentic Ghost Stories.* London: John Long, 1936.
Clutterbuck, Richard, *A True Relation of an Apparition in the Likenesse of a Bird with a White Brest, That Appeared Hovering over the Death-Beds of Some of the Children of Mr. James Oxenham.* London, 1641.
Cohen, Daniel:
*The Encyclopedia of Ghosts.* New York: Dodd, Mead, 1984.
*Ghostly Animals.* Garden City, N.Y.: Doubleday, 1977.
*Ghostly Terrors.* New York: Dodd, Mead, 1981.
*In Search of Ghosts.* New York: Dodd, Mead, 1972.
Coxe, Antony Hippisley, *Haunted Britain.* New York: McGraw-Hill, 1956.
Crowe, Catherine, *The Night Side of Nature: or, Ghosts and Ghost Seers.* Vol. 1. London: T. C. Newby, 1976.
"Dad Finds Suspect in Son's Slaying." *Chicago Sun-Times,* May 30, 1970.
David-Neel, Alexandra, *Magic and Mystery in Tibet.* Jalandhar City, India: New-Age, 1985.
Dingwall, Eric J., and Trevor H. Hall, *Four Modern Ghosts.* London: Gerald Duckworth.
"Dr. Conwell Reports Visit of Wife's Spirit." *New York Times,* December 18, 1919.
"Dr. Conwell Tells of Test of Spirit." *New York Times,* December 20, 1919.
Dorson, Richard M., *Folk Legends of Japan.* Rutland, Vt.: Charles E. Tuttle, 1981.
Evans, Hilary, *Visions, Apparitions, Alien Visitors.* Wellingborough, Northamptonshire, Great Britain: Aquarian Press, 1984.
Farson, Daniel, *The Hamlyn Book of Ghosts.* New York: Arms Press, 1970.
Finucane, R. C., *Appearances of the Dead: A Cultural History of Ghosts.* Buffalo: Prometheus Books, 1984.
Flammarion, Camille, *Death and Its Mystery.* New York: Century, 1922.
Fodor, Nandor, *The Haunted Mind: A Psychoanalyst Looks at the Supernatural.* New York: Garrett, 1963.
Forman, Joan, *Haunted Royal Homes.* London: Harrap, 1987.
Franklyn, Julian, ed., *A Survey of the Occult.* London: Arthur Barker, 1935.
Freud, Sigmund, "The Uncanny." In *Collected Papers.* Vol. 4. New York: Basic Books, 1959.
Garrett, Eileen J., ed.:
*Beyond the Five Senses.* Philadelphia: J. B. Lippincott, 1957.
*My Life as a Search for the Meaning of Mediumship.* New York: Arno Press, 1975 (reprint of 1939 edition).
Glanvill, Joseph, *Saducismus Triumphatus: or, Full and Plain Evidence Concerning Witches and Apparitions (1689).* Gainesville, Fla.: Scholars' Facsimiles & Reprints, 1966.
Godman, Colin, "Me and My Shadow." *The Unexplained* (London), Vol. 9, Issue 106.
Godman, Colin, and Lindsay St. Claire, "Seeing Double." *The Unexplained* (London), Vol. 9, Issue 108.
Green, Andrew:
*Haunted Houses.* Aylesbury, England: Shire, 1975.
*Our Haunted Kingdom.* London: Wolfe, 1973.
Green, Celia, and Charles McCreery, *Apparitions.* New York: St. Martin's Press, 1975.
Gurney, Edmund, Frederick W. H. Myers, and Frank Podmore:
*Phantasms of the Living.* 2 vols. London: Rooms of the Society for Psychical Research, 1886.
*Phantasms of the Living.* Ed. by Eleanor Mildred Sidgwick. 2 vols. New Hyde Park, N.Y.: University Books, 1962 (reprint of 1918 edition).
" 'Had Killer in My Hands,' Father of Victim Says." *Philadelphia Inquirer,* May 29, 1970.
Haining, Peter:
*A Dictionary of Ghost Lore.* Englewood Cliffs, N.J.: Prentice-Hall, 1984.
*Ghosts: The Illustrated History.* London: Sidgwick & Jackson, 1974.
Haining, Peter, ed., *The Complete Ghost Stories of Charles Dickens.* New York: Franklin Watts, 1983.
Hall, Trevor H., *The Strange Case of Edmund Gurney.* London: Gerald Duckworth, 1964.
Hallam, Jack, *Ghosts' Who's Who.* North Pomfret, Vt.: David & Charles, 1977.
Harris, Melvin, *Sorry—You've Been Duped.* London: Weidenfeld and Nicolson.
Hart, Hornell, "Man Outside His Body?" In *Beyond the Five Senses,* ed. by Eileen J. Garrett. Philadelphia: J. B. Lippincott, 1957.
Hill, Douglas, and Pat Williams, *The Supernatural.* New York: Hawthorn Books, 1965.
Hole, Christina, *Haunted England: A Survey of English Ghost-Lore.* New York: Charles Scribner's Sons, 1941.
Holms, A. Campbell, *The Facts of Psychic Science and Philosophy.* New Hyde Park, N.Y.: University Books, 1969.
Holroyd, Stuart, *Minds without Boundaries.* Garden City, N.Y.: Doubleday, 1976.
Holzer, Hans:
*The Great British Ghost Hunt.* Indianapolis: Bobbs-Merrill, 1975.
*Where the Ghosts Are.* West Nyack, N.Y.: Parker, 1973.
Hufford, David J., *The Terror That Comes in the Night.* Philadelphia: University of Pennsylvania, 1982.
Jaffé, Aniela, *Apparitions and Precognition.* New Hyde Park, N.Y.: University Books, 1963.
Jenkin, Robyn, *The New Zealand Ghost Book.* Wellington, New Zealand: A. H. & A. W. Reed, 1978.
Kiej'e, Nikolas, comp., *Japanese Grotesqueries.* Rutland, Vt.: Charles E. Tuttle, 1973.
Lang, Andrew, *The Book of Dreams and Ghosts.* New York: AMS Press, 1970 (reprint of 1897 edition).
Lavater, Ludwig, *Of Ghostes and Spirites Walking by Nyght: 1572.* Ed. by J. Dover Wilson and May Yardley. Oxford: University Press, 1929.
Lescarboura, Austin C., "Edison's Views on Life and Death." *Scientific American,* October 30, 1920.
Lethbridge, T. C., *Ghosts and the Divining-Rod.* New York: Hobbs Dorman, 1967.
Lucy, Henry W., *The Balfourian Parliament 1900-1905.* London: Hodder & Stoughton.
MacGregor, Alasdair Alpin, *The Ghost Book.* London: Ro-

bert Hale, 1955.
MacKenzie, Andrew:
*Apparitions and Ghosts: A Modern Study.* London: Arthur Barker, 1971.
*A Gallery of Ghosts: An Anthology of Reported Experience.* New York: Taplinger, 1972.
*Hauntings and Apparitions.* London: Granada, 1983.
*The Seen and the Unseen.* London: Weidenfeld and Nicolson, 1987.
*The Unexplained: Some Strange Cases in Psychical Research.* London: Arthur Barker, 1966.
McHarg, James F., "A Vision of the Aftermath of the Battle of Nechtanesmere AD 685." *Journal of the Society for Psychical Research,* December 1978.
Maher, Michaeleen, and Gertrude R. Schmeidler, "Quantitative Investigation of a Recurrent Apparition." *Journal of the American Society for Psychical Research,* October 1975.
Marsden, Simon, *The Haunted Realm: Ghosts, Spirits and Their Uncanny Abodes.* New York: E. P. Dutton, 1986.
Mather, Cotton, *On Witchcraft: Being, the Wonders of the Invisible World.* Mount Vernon, N.Y.: Peter Pauper Press, 1950 (reprint of 1692 edition).
Myers, F. W. H., *Human Personality and Its Survival of Bodily Death.* Ed. by Susy Smith. New Hyde Park, N.Y.: University Books, 1961.
Neuer, Roni, and Herbert Libertson, *Ukiyo-E: 250 Years of Japanese Art.* New York: Mayflower Books, 1979.
O'Donnell, Elliott:
*Animal Ghosts: or, Animal Hauntings and the Hereafter.* London: William Rider & Son, 1913.
*Casebook of Ghosts.* Ed. by Harry Ludlam. London: W. Foulsham, 1969.
*Family Ghosts and Ghostly Phenomena.* New York: E. P. Dutton, 1934.
*Great Ghost Stories: Omnibus Edition.* Ed. by Harry Ludlam. New York: Arco, 1984.
*Haunted Churches.* London: Quality Press, 1939.
Osis, Karlis, *Deathbed Observations by Physicians and Nurses.* New York: Parapsychology Foundation, 1961.
Owen, Robert Dale, *Footfalls on the Boundary of Another World.* Philadelphia: J. B. Lippincott, 1860.
Paine, Lauran, *A Gaggle of Ghosts.* London: Robert Hale, 1971.
Price, Harry, *The End of Borley Rectory: 'The Most Haunted House in England.'* London: George G. Harrap, 1946.
Prince, Walter Franklin, *Noted Witnesses for Psychic Occurrences.* New Hyde Park, N.Y.: University Books, 1963.
Rank, Otto, *The Double.* Ed. and transl. by Harry Tucker, Jr. Chapel Hill: University of North Carolina Press, 1971.
Raudive, Konstantin, *Breakthrough: An Amazing Experiment in Electronic Communication with the Dead.* Ed. by Joyce Morton, transl. by Nadia Fowler. Gerrards Cross, England: Colin Smythe, 1971.
Redgrove, H. Stanley, and I. M. L. Redgrove, *Joseph Glanvill and Psychical Research in the Seventeenth Century.* London: William Rider, 1921.
Rhine, Louisa E., *The Invisible Picture: A Study of Psychic Experiences.* Jefferson, N.C.: McFarland, 1981.
Rogo, D. Scott, *An Experience of Phantoms.* New York: Taplinger, 1974.
Russell, Eric, *Ghosts.* London: B. T. Batsford, 1970.
Salter, W. H., *Zoar (Perspectives in Psychical Research).* New York: Arno Press, 1975.
Schatzman, Morton:
"Ghosts in the Machine." *Psychology Today,* January 1981.
"Living with Apparitions." *New York Times Magazine,* April 27, 1980.
*The Story of Ruth.* New York: G. P. Putnam's Sons, 1980.
Schaller, George B., and Millicent E. Selsam, *The Tiger: Its Life in the Wild.* New York: Harper & Row, 1969.
Shackleton, Ernest, *South: The Story of Shackleton's 1914-1917 Expedition.* London: Heinemann, 1970.
Shepard, Leslie, ed., *Encyclopedia of Occultism & Parapsychology.* 3 vols. Detroit: Gale Research, 1984.
Shirley, Ralph, *The Mystery of the Human Double.* New Hyde Park, N.Y.: University Books, 1965.
Simon, Seymour, *Ghosts.* Philadelphia: J. B. Lippincott, 1976.
Smith, Susy, *Prominent American Ghosts.* Cleveland: World, 1967.
Smyth, Frank, and Roy Stemman, Mysteries of the Afterlife. London: Aldus Books, 1978.
Spalding, Thomas Alfred, *Elizabethan Demonology.* Norwood, Penn.: Norwood Editions, 1975 (reprint of 1880 edition).
Stemman, Roy, "A Thoroughly Modern Medium." *The Unexplained* (London), Vol. 9, Issue 100.
Stevenson, John, *Yoshitoshi's Thirty-Six Ghosts.* New York: Weatherhill, 1983.
Tabori, Paul, *Harry Price: The Biography of a Ghost-Hunter.* London: Athenaeum Press, 1950.
Thompson, C. J. S., *The Mystery and Lore of Apparitions.* Detroit: Gale Research, 1974 (reprint of 1931 edition).
Timbs, John:
*Predictions Realized in Modern Times.* Ann Arbor, Mich.: Gryphon Books, 1971 (reprint of 1880 edition).
*Signs before Death.* London: William Tegg, 1875.
Tweedie, Geo. R., "Gossip about Ghosts: A Lecture to Accompany a Series of 50 Lantern Transparencies." Unpublished pamphlet, no date.
Trevelyan, Marie, *Folk-Lore and Folk Stories of Wales.* Norwood, Penn.: Norwood Editions, 1973.
Tyrrell, G. N. M., *Apparitions.* London: Gerald Duckworth, 1953.
Underwood, Peter:
*A Gazetteer of British Ghosts.* New York: Walker, 1975.
*The Ghost Hunter's Guide.* Poole, England: Blandford Press, 1986.
*The Ghost Hunters: Who They Are and What They Do.* London: Robert Hale, 1985.
*Haunted London.* London: Harrap, 1973.
Upward, Allen, *Secrets of the Past.* London: Alston Rivers, 1909.
Walker, Danton, *I Believe in Ghosts.* New York: Taplinger, 1969.
Walker, G. A., *Gatherings from Grave Yards.* London: Longman, 1839.
Wereide, Thorstein, "Norway's Human Doubles." In *Beyond the Five Senses,* ed. by Eileen J. Garrett. Philadelphia: J. B. Lippincott, 1957.
Whitaker, Terence W., *Yorkshire's Ghosts and Legends.* London: Granada, 1983.
Whitfield, A. G. W., "Physician to the Prince of Wales." *Journal of the Royal College of Physicians of London,* October 1983.
Wilson, John Dover, comp., *Life in Shakespeare's England: A Book of Elizabethan Prose.* Folcroft, Penn.: Folcroft Library Editions, 1976 (reprint of 1913 edition).
Wolman, Benjamin B., ed., *Handbook of Parapsychology.* New York: Van Nostrand Rheinhold, 1977.
Zorab, G., "Have We to Reckon with a Special Phantom-Forming Predisposition?" *Journal of the Society for Psychical Research,* March 1975.

## PICTURE CREDITS

*The sources for the pictures in this book are listed below. Credits for pictures shown from left to right are separated by semicolons; credits for pictures shown from top to bottom are separated by dashes.*

Cover: Art by John Rush. 7: Simon Marsden, London, detail from pages 16, 17. 8-17: Simon Marsden, London. 19: Art by Wendy Popp. 20: Art by Lisa Semerad. 22: British Library, London; Trustees of the British Museum, London. 25: Mary Evans Picture Library, London/Society for Psychical Research, London. 28, 29: Mary Evans Picture Library, London. 31: From *Ghosts and Hauntings,* by Dennis Bardens, Taplinger Publishing Co., New York, 1968. Reprinted by permission. 34: Mary Evans Picture Library, London. 37: Art by Bryan Leister, detail from page 41. 38-45: Art by Bryan Leister. 47: Art by Wendy Popp. 48: Trustees of the British Museum, London; from *Of Ghostes and Spirites Walking by Nyght 1572,* by Ludwig Lavater, printed for Shakespeare Association, University Press, Oxford, 1929. 50, 51: Paintings by Studio of Van Dyke, courtesy National Portrait Gallery, London. 53: Photo by Bryan and Cherry Alexander, © 1982 Time-Life Books, B.V., from *Peoples of the Wild: Masked Dancers of West Africa: The Dogon.* 54: Eric Valli, Saint-Jorioz, France. 55: Richard Riddell. 56, 57: Stephen Pern, Hastings, Sussex. 59: Mary Evans Picture Library, London. 60: Art by Bruce Sharp. 62: From *Animals: 1419 Copyright-free Illustrations of Mammals, Birds, Fish, Insects, etc.,* selected by Jim Harter, Dover Publications, New York, 1979. 64: Eddowes/*Philadelphia Inquirer*/Temple Urban Archives. 67: Photographic images reproduced from the original, Conwellana-Templana Collection, Temple University Libraries. 70, 71: Courtesy Sara Schneidman; Mary Evans Picture Library, London/Society for Psychical Research; courtesy Sara Schneidman. 73: Print by Utagawa Kunisada, Spencer Museum of Art, University of Kansas, photographed by Jon Blumb, detail from pages 78, 79. 74, 75: Print by Utagawa Kuniyoshi, Spencer Museum of Art, University of Kansas, photographed by Jon Blumb. 76: Print by Tsukioka Yoshitoshi, Collection of Mr. and Mrs. Marc F. Wilson, Kansas City, photograph courtesy Spencer Museum of Art, University of Kansas, photographed by Jon Blumb. 77: Print by Shunkōsai Hokuei, Spencer Museum of

Art, University of Kansas, photographed by Jon Blumb. 78, 79: Print by Utagawa Kunisada, Spencer Museum of Art, University of Kansas, photographed by Jon Blumb. 80, 81: Print by Utagawa Kuniyoshi, Spencer Museum of Art, University of Kansas, photographed by Jon Blumb. 83: Art by Wendy Popp. 84: Fresco by Pinturicchio, courtesy Musei Vaticani, Rome, photograph by Scala, Florence. 86, 87 photomontage: Background courtesy Sir Benjamin Stone Collection, reproduced by permission of House of Commons Library, London. Figures, Sir Benjamin Stone Collection, courtesy National Portrait Gallery, London. 88: Courtesy National Portrait Gallery, London, silver print by Larry Sherer. 90: Painting by Joseph Karl Stieler, Neue Pinakothek, Munich, photograph by Joachim Blauel/Artothek, silver print by Larry Sherer. 91: Painting by A. Curran, courtesy National Portrait Gallery, London, silver print by Larry Sherer. 92, 93: City of Vienna Burial Museum. 96: Granger Collection—from *L'Optique* by Fulgence Marion, published by Librairie Hachette, Paris, 1874. 98: Courtesy Fondation Alexandra David-Neel, Digne-les-Bains, France. 101: Roger-Viollet, Paris. 102, 103: Crown Copyright, reproduced with permission of the Controller of Her Majesty's Stationery Office and the Board of Trustees of the Armouries, Tower of London; based on official chart, Tower of London, by Don Pottinger, published by Elm Tree Books, London, © 1978. 104-109: Details based on official chart, Tower of London, by Don Pottinger, published by Elm Tree Books, London, © 1978. Figures by Allen Davis. 111: Art by Wendy Popp. 112: Library of Congress; National Portrait Gallery, Smithsonian Institution, Washington, D.C. (NPG M.81.1). 113: Courtesy Kunhardt Collection. 115: Courtesy Margaret Minney, Waresley, Cambridgeshire. 116: Popperfoto, London. 117: Courtesy Colin Smythe Limited, Gerrards Cross, Buckinghamshire—Bild/Mietz, Hamburg. 118: RAF Museum, London. 120, 121 photomontage: Courtesy the Raymond Mander and Joe Mitchenson Theatre Collection, London. Figure © Time-Life Books. 122: Bulloz, Paris—from *The Ghosts of Versailles*, by Lucille Iremonger, Faber & Faber, London, 1957 (2). 124, 125: Crivello, Moncalieri, courtesy Conte Augusto Olivero Grimaldi, Moncalieri, ghosts courtesy Conte Augusto Olivero Grimaldi, Moncalieri. 126: Harry Price Library, University of London. 127: Mary Evans Picture Library, London/Harry Price Collection, University of London. 129: Art by Lloyd K. Townsend, detail from pages 132, 133. 130-139: Art by Lloyd K. Townsend.

# INDEX

*Numerals in italics indicate an illustration of the subject mentioned.*

Time-Life Books Inc.
is a wholly owned subsidiary of
**TIME INCORPORATED**



*The Consultant:*
Marcello Truzzi, professor of sociology at Eastern Michigan University, is also director of the Center for Scientific Anomalies Research (CSAR) and editor of its journal, the *Zetetic Scholar.* Dr. Truzzi, who considers himself a "constructive skeptic" with regard to claims of the paranormal, works through the CSAR to produce dialogues between critics and proponents of unusual scientific claims.

*Other Publications:*

TIME-LIFE BOOKS

TIME FRAME
FIX IT YOURSELF
FITNESS, HEALTH & NUTRITION
SUCCESSFUL PARENTING
HEALTHY HOME COOKING
UNDERSTANDING COMPUTERS
LIBRARY OF NATIONS
THE ENCHANTED WORLD
THE KODAK LIBRARY OF CREATIVE PHOTOGRAPHY
GREAT MEALS IN MINUTES
THE CIVIL WAR
PLANET EARTH
COLLECTOR'S LIBRARY OF THE CIVIL WAR
THE EPIC OF FLIGHT
THE GOOD COOK
WORLD WAR II
HOME REPAIR AND IMPROVEMENT
THE OLD WEST

*For information on and a full description of any of the Time-Life Books series listed above, please call 1-800-621-7026 or write:*
Reader Information
Time-Life Customer Service
P.O. Box C-32068
Richmond, Virginia 23261-2068

This volume is one of a series that examines the history and nature of seemingly paranormal phenomena. Other books in the series include:
*Mystic Places*
*Psychic Powers*
*The UFO Phenomenon*
*Psychic Voyages*

**Library of Congress Cataloging in Publication Data**
Phantom encounters / by the editors of Time-Life Books.
p. cm. (Mysteries of the unknown).
Bibliography: p.
Includes index.
ISBN 0-8094-6328-8. ISBN 0-8094-6329-6 (lib. bdg.)
1. Apparitions. 2. Ghosts
I. Time-Life Books. II. Series.
BF.P45 1988
133.1—dc19 87-29125 CIP


First printing. Printed in U.S.A.
Published simultaneously in Canada.
School and library distribution by Silver Burdett Company, Morristown, New Jersey 07960.